LONG WAY BACK TO THE
RIVER KWAI

LONG WAY BACK TO THE
RIVER KWAI

A Harrowing True Story
of Survival in
World War II

LOET VELMANS

Arcade Publishing • New York

For Edith

Arcade Publishing books may be purchased in bulk at special discounts for sales promotion, corporate gifts, fund-raising, or educational purposes. Special editions can also be created to specifications. For details, contact the Special Sales Department, Arcade Publishing, 307 West 36th Street, 11th Floor, New York, NY 10018 or info@skyhorsepublishing.com.

Arcade Publishing® is a registered trademark of Skyhorse Publishing, Inc.®, a Delaware corporation.

Visit our website at www.arcadepub.com.

10 9 8 7 6 5 4 3 2

Library of Congress Cataloging-in-Publication Data is available on file.

ISBN: 978-1-61145-185-6

Printed in the United States of America

Contents

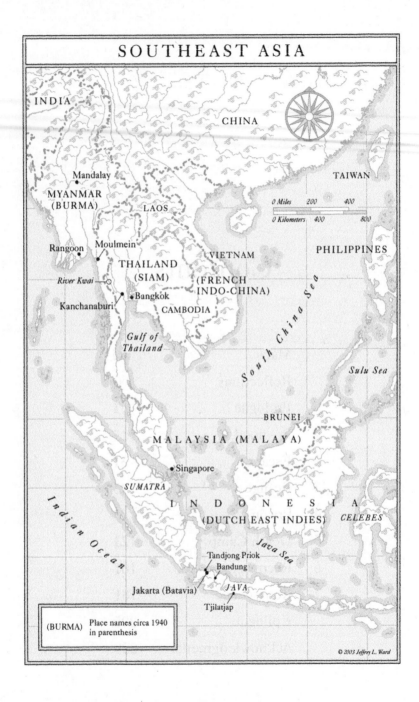

SOUTHEAST ASIA

INDIA

CHINA

TAIWAN

Mandalay

MYANMAR
(BURMA)

LAOS

0 Miles 200 400

0 Kilometers 400 800

Rangoon   Moulmein

VIETNAM

PHILIPPINES

River Kwai

THAILAND
(SIAM)

(FRENCH
INDO-CHINA)

Kanchanaburi   •Bangkok

CAMBODIA

*Gulf of
Thailand*

South China Sea

Sulu Sea

BRUNEI

MALAYSIA (MALAYA)

•Singapore

SUMATRA

I N D O N E S I A

Indian Ocean

(DUTCH EAST INDIES)

CELEBES

Java Sea

Tandjong Priok
Bandung

Jakarta (Batavia)

JAVA

Tjilatjap

(BURMA)   Place names circa 1940
in parenthesis

© 2003 Jeffrey L. Ward

SIAM-BURMA RAILWAY

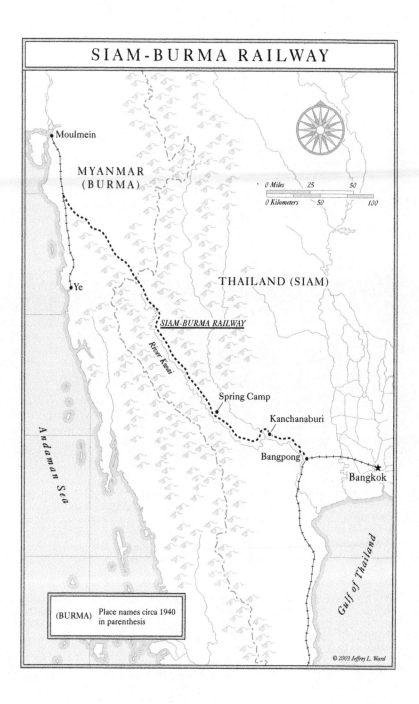

Moulmein

MYANMAR
(BURMA)

THAILAND (SIAM)

0 Miles   25   50
0 Kilometers   50   100

Ye

SIAM-BURMA RAILWAY

River Kwai

Andaman Sea

Spring Camp

Kanchanaburi

Bangpong

Bangkok

Gulf of Thailand

| (BURMA) | Place names circa 1940 in parenthesis |

© 2003 Jeffrey L. Ward

LONG WAY BACK TO THE
RIVER KWAI

Reflections

Japan has often abundantly deserved the world's empathy and compassion for its endurance of earthquakes and other natural disasters. The country's first recorded major earthquake dates back to the year 684 AD. Since then, more than forty major quakes have decimated cities, villages, and countryside. In our modern time, with its instant worldwide coverage, we have witnessed the great Kobe earthquake of 1995 and its successor, 2011's earthquake, tsunami, and nuclear disaster. The devastating television images from Japan have inspired universal respect and admiration for the way the Japanese people respond to adversity. What is it in the Japanese character that gives rise to such a disciplined reaction to a succession of disasters? Japan experts and legions of pundits are called on to spout their views about the heroic and stoic Japanese. Even in wary China and Korea, traditional competitors who have always been suspicious of Japan, the Japanese Empire's reaction to catastrophe is admired and held up as a model.

For me, the repercussions of such disasters pose a dilemma. How do I reconcile Japan's sterling character with the utterly ruthless and cruel behavior that I experienced during my three-and-a-half-year stint as a starved and beaten prisoner of war during World War II? Now, it seems, the grandchildren of the Japanese soldiers who brought so much pain and grief to their prisoners have become the world's models of self-sacrificing behavior. Should I now feel different? I never did manage to engage with any Japanese persons of my generation to discuss what happened in the war from our opposing perspectives. So I have always remained suspicious of their dealings and motives. Has the time arrived for me to become more tolerant, especially of the post-war generations? Can I finally bring myself to forgive the brutal beating, the starvation, the disease, and the deaths of my friends?

My preoccupation with Japan started over half a century ago, a month or two before the Japanese attack on Pearl Harbor. The white minority in the Dutch East Indies, among whom I had landed early in the war, had lived a sheltered life for generations. Now, as tensions between Japan and the West increased, the Dutch colonial community—a homogeneous group of expatriates—became nervous about its future. Internal tensions, fueled by apprehension, intensified when the Pacific War erupted. As a seventeen-year-old, living in Java, I wasn't aware of the strengths and weaknesses of our army, but I did not share the colonials' complacent (and racist) conviction that the Japanese would easily be defeated. Once I was drafted, I grew increasingly skeptical of our army's chances to withstand the inevitable invasion.

The war years were filled with hatred.

Even after the war, I continued to have Japan on my mind. My old fury flared up again when I read about the Tokyo War Crimes trials where, I felt, so many leading Japanese officials and military brass escaped harsh punishment. For many years I was haunted by two questions: Who are these people? And what drives them?

It is nearly impossible to define a culture, whether foreign or one's own. The subject is too complicated. The only supposition I can advance, tired as it may be, is that the Japanese have a greater sense of cohesion than any Western nation. This may be stating the obvious, especially since it concerns such a homogeneous population, where immigrants represent just 2 percent of the population. Yet we cannot help but make comparisons between the Japanese and ourselves. This has led to a pattern of questionable conclusions. Japanese stoicism under stress shouldn't be considered a miracle: in Japan, self-discipline is derived from a common conviction that the goals of the nation precede the well-being of the individual. Japanese unity equals fealty to the tribe, a striving toward a common goal, and, when the historical occasion demands, the sharing of sacrifice. This comes out strongly in times of natural disaster and nuclear catastrophe. It also applies, with a vengeance, to the political enemy as well as the foreign business competitor. It explains the treatment of the dishonored and dishonorable prisoners of war, and the barely tolerated minorities such as the Korean immigrants. The hopes and the ambitions of the Japanese individual play a secondary role.

In my slowly dawning understanding of the Japanese, I have begun to comprehend how the nation religiously, even fanatically, came to believe that it was the West that had started World War II. The Emperor and his leadership had so ordained. Japanese society was an edifice in which all decisions made from the top were slavishly obeyed. There was no tolerance for the idea that initiatives could germinate at the bottom and work their way to the top. As a result, for many generations, the homeland had become a sacred shrine, which in war needed to be defended to the last man, woman, and child. In the Japanese concept of honor, no soldier could contemplate surrender: from the kamikaze pilot to the Japanese soldier fighting in the battle of Okinawa and other islands, suicide was the only option. It also explained to me that the 1945 surrender, ordered by the Emperor, resulted in the complete acceptance of the American occupation. Obedience meant not only cooperation with the occupying American forces, but also no reexamination of one's own conduct during the war, resulting in the (mystifying to Westerners) attitude that no apology for wartime misdeeds was required.

REFLECTIONS

To believe that Japan's unique character will ever change is an illusion. For me, an ex-POW writing this almost seventy years after my imprisonment, Japan still fascinates. At times it will seem admirable; at others it will be frightening, possibly hateful. It remains on my mind, with all its strengths, weaknesses, and ambiguities.

Loet Velmans
Sheffield, Massachusetts
May 2011

Prologue

I WANTED TO FIND SPRING CAMP, where, fifty-seven years ago, I nearly died. I wanted to revisit the jungle where my friend George's bones lay buried.

George was not the last of my friends to die, but the memory of his death was the one that settled itself into the inside of one of my brain cells over fifty years ago and has remained there ever since. I buried George hastily, yanking and pushing his arms and legs unceremoniously in order to stuff him into the burlap sack that served as his coffin. It was 1943. George and I had been bunkmates, working side by side on the Thailand-Burma railroad, the "Railway of Death," as slave laborers and prisoners of war of the Japanese. We were famished, beaten, emaciated, and diseased.

George was twenty-seven years old and had been a plantation manager in the Dutch East Indies before the war. His health had been failing for several months, and he had given up the will to live. Despite his weakened state, the Japanese guards would drive him out of our hut every morning to his labor detail. "They won't let me go," he had said to me over and over before the malaria-induced dementia set in. But it was his last hour that made his death unforgettable: his babbling gibberish; his pale, bloated stomach horribly swollen with beriberi; his mottled limbs gouged to the bone by gangrenous ulcers; and, finally, those piercing shrieks and deep moans of anger, pain, and despair.

I was seventeen years old when the Germans invaded my native Holland. I became a fugitive, an escape artist, always one step ahead of the enemy, until he caught up with me on the island of Java. Even though I started off fleeing from the Nazis, the enemy I came to know intimately had a Japanese face: impassive, masklike. I spent my POW years trying to figure out what lay behind that brutal mask: what made this enemy tick. It has only been in recent years, when I started thinking about writing this book, that I realized that much of my life since the war has been spent trying to understand the Japanese.

For years I thought about going back to Thailand. But each time that I planned a trip there with my wife Edith, some more urgent event in our lives resulted in the sort of postponement that lasts from year to year, decade to decade. I suppose I was suffering from a lingering reluctance to face memories of the blackest time of my life. Finally, in

February 2000, I could put it off no longer. Edith and I were on our way from New York to Kanchanaburi, about ninety miles west of Bangkok, to meet up with a fellow POW survivor and good friend, Lex Noyon. Lex, a retired professor in the social sciences, had flown in from his home in Amsterdam. It was Lex who had whetted my appetite for this trip, for he had visited the river Kwai several times. On his last visit, some ten years earlier, he had bicycled off the main road and found a spot in the bush that he recognized and identified as Spring Camp, one of the forty-odd encampments along the Thailand-Burma railroad, where over 20,000 British, Australian, Dutch, and American POWs and an estimated 200,000 Asian slave laborers were worked to death.

I wasn't expecting much: I knew that all traces of our camp had been swallowed up by the jungle. After the war, the Thais themselves had destroyed most of the railway — trade with Burma had not been important enough to justify a rail link with a nation that was historically prone to invade its neighbor. I knew that in recent years Thailand's rapid economic development had further changed the landscape — large stretches of jungle had been cleared into lush farmland, suburbs, soccer fields, and vast golf courses.

We had arranged for a car and driver, but we soon discovered that our "guide" neither spoke nor understood any Western language. We were well provided with maps, but these were of little help in pinpointing the exact location of our camp. We started out driving north from Kanchana-buri, on a modern two-lane highway. Two and a half hours later, we were becoming increasingly frustrated, for any attempt at communication with our driver — we thought an earlier turnoff would have brought us nearer to our destination — was met with no response. He was determined to take us to the place he had decided we must visit: a picturesque waterfall, visited by tour buses and groups of Thai families who had spread out blankets and picnics among the trees.

No, no, we indicated, this was not it. Off we drove again, at breakneck speed. Our pleas to go a little slower met with stone-faced incomprehension. Then, unexpectedly, our driver veered off the main road and screeched to a stop in front of a modern building on a green, densely wooded hillside in the middle of the tropical wilderness.

"Welcome to Hellfire Pass Memorial." A strong handshake accompanied the hearty booming Australian voice. He was tall, heavily built, khaki clad, and introduced himself as Terry Beaton, the manager of the memorial, a museum funded by the Australian government, corporations, and private individuals that had been completed in 1998. When Beaton, a retired lieutenant colonel in the Australian army, heard about our quest, he was delighted. "Most of our visitors have been the children or grandchildren of POWs, but you two are the genuine article. You are the first Dutch POWs I have met. Welcome indeed."

Beaton took us down the mountain on a newly constructed concrete walkway to a clearing in the jungle where the railway had been restored to its original state, using fifty-year-old railroad ties, which are commonly known as sleepers. We walked for about an hour in the hot and humid midday sun through Hellfire Pass, a narrow, seventy-five-foot-deep gorge that had been carved out of the rock by slave labor. We remembered how we had been teamed up to hammer long spikes into the rock by hand, to make holes deep enough for blasting. Beaton, a railroad engineer by profession, greatly admired the scope of the enterprise. "You have to give the Japanese credit," he said. "They built a three-hundred-mile-long railroad without the benefit of proper equipment, in fifteen months, through this kind of mountainous jungle terrain. And in the rainy season, this is one of the worst climate zones in the whole world. It's a feat equal to the construction of the Egyptian pyramids."

"And like the pharaohs," observed Lex dryly, "they didn't give a fig what it cost in human lives."

Our new friend began speculating what had made Lex and me survivors. "You aren't very big fellows," he said. "Every prisoner received the same miserable rations. If you were tall and heavy, with a bigger body to feed, you'd be the first to run out of gas."

At Hellfire Pass, he told us, the natural animosity between the Brits and their Aussie cousins had given rise to a fierce contest: which side could drill the most holes. The lackadaisical Dutch, working at the slowest pace they could, despite the beatings they brought on themselves for not working fast enough, stayed out of the competition, saved their strength, and enjoyed a higher survival rate.

At a spot near the end of the clearing, work was in progress on the reconstruction of a wooden bridge across a ravine, where dozens of POWs had fallen to their deaths. Sixty-nine others were believed to have been beaten to death there by their guards.

Armed with refreshed memories and new directions — in Thai, for our driver — Lex and I were more determined than ever to find our own camp. And finally we did achieve our goal. At the end of a dirt road riddled with deep potholes, we came to a small clearing. Our driver jumped out of the car and took off in a hurry, leaving us to scratch our heads. We were relieved to see him return a short while later, gesturing to us to follow him on a narrow trail. After a few minutes we arrived at another picturesque clearing beside a pond. A large handwritten sign read NATURAL SPRING. There was no sign of human habitation, but within a few minutes we were surrounded by little children, who seemed to spring out of nowhere. The children were enthralled when my wife offered to let them look at themselves on the screen of her digital video camera.

Lex doubted that we were in the right spot. Although it was true that Spring Camp had been named after a nearby spring, the other markers had disappeared. The last time he had visited the spot, there had been a small bridge. Muttering to himself, Lex walked off, leaving Edith and me to admire the beautiful children, who were making faces and laughing at themselves in the mirror of Edith's camera. After about ten minutes, I grew apprehensive. Lex, the intrepid seventy-six-year-old traveler, suffered from glaucoma and a bad heart. I went after him and was relieved when I heard a distant response to my repeated calls. I reached him standing on the edge of a large open field with a clear view of a low mountain range not too far away.

"This is it," he said. "It's the same spot where I stood eight years ago, even though the small bridge that was here before has disappeared. Look at those two stone formations on the mountain, which we could only see in those mornings when the rain stopped." I had no recollection of the bridge, nor of the stone formations, but I did remember that I had been too sick and weak to admire any scenery. Standing in that pristine spot in the middle of nowhere, calm and lovely and empty. I felt no emotion. So this is it, I thought. And that's all there is to it. I looked around perfunctorily to see if I could see any artifact, any sign of human habitation. But there was nothing. Spring Camp had been swallowed up by time. "Come on, Lex, let's go," I said impatiently.

It wasn't until we were seated in the car, driving back to our hotel after a long and tiring day, that I felt something — some of the old fear and the old anger stirring.

Startled, I recalled our first day in Kananchaburi, when we had visited the famous "Bridge over the River Kwai," one of the area's major tourist attractions. Dozens of hotels and rooming houses had sprung up together with souvenir stands; craft exhibits; street merchants hawking clothing, scarves, hats, and postcards; food stalls; restaurants; and all the other paraphernalia of the tourist trade. That restored railway bridge — the only survivor of the railway's three steel and sixty-six wooden bridges — was apparently a popular destination for Japanese tourists, who, we were told, visited this area in large numbers, attracted by the easily accessible and inexpensive golf courses. The bridge rose high above the water, its rails perched on a narrow track on which it was wise to move forward no more than two abreast, slowly and cautiously. As we walked across, groups of Japanese passed us from the opposite side. They seemed impervious to any risk to themselves or anyone else in their path. Small square platforms had been built every few yards to give pedestrians room to let each other pass, but the Japanese did not avail themselves of these. They would not step out of their way to let us through, but barreled onward in groups of twenty or more, leaving us quaking on the sidelines. Edith and I would wait until we saw an opportunity to make a quick dash to the next platform; Lex, who could hardly see two steps ahead, blithely walked on, forcing the Japanese to stop in their tracks for a second, even though they would not yield. Edith grabbed my hand and said she was a little scared; I felt more irritated than anything else. We didn't see the Japanese paying any attention to the memorials along the bank of the river. They were too busy filming and photographing each other with the river as background. But now, in the car, my irritation swelled to anger — at myself as much as at the Japanese. How long would I continue to let these people walk all over me? Had nothing changed?

That same night we had dinner in a charming restaurant that also floated on a deck in the river. The light of a full moon was reflected in the water. The whole scene was calm and peaceful and could not be less reminiscent of the way the banks along the river had looked half a century ago. Japan's domination was far away and long ago.

A quiet hush hung over the restaurant. Occasionally a tourist barge with glittering lights would glide by; its thin sounds, in various tones and different languages, evaporated into the starlit night. Suddenly a commotion right next to our restaurant disturbed our tranquillity. A poorly lit vessel docked next to us and was quickly populated by a large group of Japanese. A voice started to blare through a shrill sound system, and then the music started. After about ten minutes of deafening noise, the floating disco cast off from its landing and clucked away. The sound of Japanese rock music and the harsh commands of the disc jockey drifted away. In the taxi on the way back, Lex managed to calm my anger. "This is my twelfth visit to Thailand," he said. "I have met many young Japanese. The new generation. They want to know what happened. They don't say it openly, but they don't seem to trust what their elders tell them about the war." Who was I to say what the Japanese made of their visit to the bridge? They too had lost thousands of men on the railway and tens of thousands in Burma. Were they here to honor the fallen? To communicate with the souls of their dead fathers and grandfathers? On the bridge, when they moved massively toward us, was it a rekindling of their anger and disdain for the Westerners they held responsible for a war that, they believed, had been forced upon them? For the unforgivable act of the atomic destruction of Hiroshima and Nagasaki?

For some reason, I found myself thinking about a bathtub I had once been in on one of my visits to Tokyo. It was in 1980: from the 1950s through the mid-1980s, I traveled to Tokyo frequently on business. On this occasion, the Dutch ambassador and his wife, Johan and Nan Kaufmann, who were old friends, had invited me to stay with them in the Netherlands' embassy. The building was designed in the 1920s in an orientalized Anglo-Western style, a modest but elegant villa in the heart of Japan's capital.

The bathtub was the longest one I had ever been in. Fully stretched, I could practically paddle back and forth. My kimono lay neatly folded on a wooden stool near the door; I had tried to hang it up but hadn't been able to reach the metal hook. The unusual size of the tub and the lofty placement of the hook seemed designed for giants. The Japanese builder who built it, years before the postwar influx of Westerners into Tokyo, must have estimated the average Dutchman to be twice as tall as the average Japanese. I had seen Japanese prints depicting the sixteenth-century Dutch explorers who set up a trading post in Nagasaki: they looked like alien Goliaths. Four hundred years later, it seemed to me, we were still about as clueless about each other as we had been then. Two other images came to me as I lay there in that bathtub: an illustration of my boyhood copy of *Gulliver's Travels,* showing a giant Gulliver trussed up by dozens of scurrying ant-sized figures; and the famous 1945 photograph of victor and vanquished — a tall General MacArthur towering over a diminutive Emperor Hirohito.

Throughout my life I have lived in many countries and traveled in many environments. I quickly feel at home everywhere. But in Japan it was different. I was acutely aware of the differences. I always sensed that the Japanese businessmen and government officials I met did not feel comfortable around me either, nor around other Westerners. And it makes no difference, I thought, that they have no inkling that I was their prisoner, working in Thailand, on the Burma railway, in World War II.

On our last day in Thailand, we visited the Allied war graves in Kanchanaburi. In a large field surrounded by trees, thousands of simple crosses identified the graves of prisoners buried here. We wandered up and down the rows of graves, trying to find the names of our comrades. Most of those buried here were between the ages of twenty and twenty-three. In the Dutch section Lex discovered the name of a boy he had gone to school with almost seventy years ago. I was hoping to find my friend George's name, for I knew that many of those interred here had been moved from the individual camp graveyards shortly after the war. But there were just too many graves, too many names. It was impossible to find anyone I knew.

Meanwhile Edith had walked to the far side of the cemetery, where a group of workmen were digging up a row of beautiful trees. She was curious to know why. One of the men, dressed like the others, lifted his conical hat and explained, in unvarnished Australian, that the trees were dying and needed to be replaced. They started to chat, and Edith mentioned that those two men at the other side of the graveyard were her husband and his friend, and that they had both been in the area as POWs.

The man was Rod Beattie, supervisor of Allied war graves in Thailand. Beattie had lived and worked in the area for twelve years and was among the original builders of the memorial at Hellfire Pass. Like Terry Beaton, he was a railroad engineer, and he was equally passionate about the history of "his" railway. He had walked the entire three-hundred-mile trail several times and talked like an archaeologist: on frequent expeditions alongside and on the overgrown railway bed, he would still dig up spikes, tools, and the occasional human bone. He too was excited to meet two Dutch ex-POWs, and he took us back to his office to inspect his collection of artifacts and examine old

World War II aerial reconnaissance photographs of the area. When we pointed to the location of Spring Camp on our map, Beattie assured us that we had been in the right place: "I've been there several times," he told us. "That's where I found some human bones."

George, I thought. Now we can go home.

1

Boyhood

I WAS TEN YEARS OLD IN 1933, the year Hitler came to power. During my teens, as Hitler's grand plan to expand the Third Reich began to be realized, my parents and their friends were confident that, whatever else might happen in Europe, the Germans would leave the Netherlands alone, as they had done in World War I.

My parents, like their parents before them, had been born and bred in Amsterdam's Jewish community. Amsterdam had been home to a significant and often influential Jewish population since the sixteenth century. Jews fleeing the Spanish Inquisition, although not necessarily welcomed with open arms, were allowed to practice their religion by the Dutch, who have always had an innate tolerance for people of different religious and political persuasions.

By the time I was born, families like ours — descendants of a second wave of Jewish immigrants who had arrived from Germany and Eastern Europe in the late eighteenth century — had been totally assimilated into Dutch society. For us, Yom Kippur was the only day of the Jewish calendar on which we acknowledged our faith and stayed home from work or school. Even then my parents and I did not attend services, and we fasted only until we felt hungry. We were linked to our Jewish forefathers primarily through the four great rituals of life: circumcision, bar mitzvah, marriage, and burial. On our birth certificates, however, we were identified as Jews, and thereby inexorably classified as members unto death of the Nederlandsch Israelitische Gemeenschap (the Dutch Jewish Religious Community). In the Netherlands the religious affiliation of all citizens was officially listed. Each head of a Dutch household who belonged to a church or synagogue found on his annual income tax form an obligatory small assessment for the government-imposed "church" tax, the proceeds of which supported one's assigned denomination. Holland is a neat country, and the Dutch are a precise people who file each subject in its proper place. In a precomputer era, all pertinent personal information about each and every citizen and resident — name, address, sex, age, and religion — was recorded on endless lists and efficiently stored in file cabinets and boxes. The Nazis got the lot.

Both of my parents had left school at age twelve or thirteen. My mother (a woman ahead of her time) was a buyer and department head at the Bijenkorf (the beehive),

Holland's largest department store. Her job frequently took her to Europe's fashion capitals, leaving me in the care of our live-in housekeeper. I was used to the fact that Mother came home late and left early, but comparing myself to my friends whose mothers were there for them all the time made me feel a little distant and apart. On her return from abroad, Mother overcompensated for her absences by smothering me with love and concern — and the latest fashions for boys. I tried to get out of wearing the Parisian sailor suits and the cashmere vests she brought back for me. I did not want to be the best-dressed kid on the block. I couldn't stand being decked out in my Sunday best and would change my clothes as soon as my parents were out of the house. My father was in the fur trade. I was always excited when he took me to his office which was located in the "House of the Seven Heads," a historic building on one of Amsterdam's canals.

Every evening would find me sprawled full length on the living room floor, the pages of the newspaper spread out in front of me, brooding over the state of the world. I was obsessed with the political turbulence in Europe. Another victory for Hitler: the Saarland, the Rhineland, Austria, Czechoslovakia. Meanwhile Italy was overrunning Abyssinia, and Franco was winning the Spanish Civil War. On the other side of the world, the Japanese were carving off ever larger chunks of China; banner headlines reported on the Rape of Nanking. But Asia was too far for me to worry about. It was what was going on in Germany, our country's next-door neighbor, that really mattered. Reading about the imprisonment of those who opposed the Nazis in concentration camps and the persecution of the German Jews made my blood boil.

I went to the cinema at least once a week. There, before the main feature, Fox MovieTone would show footage of Hitler and his awesome hordes of brown-shirted SS men. The sight of Hitler's followers roaring in unison and raising their right arms sent a chill down my spine. How can they let him get away with it? I'd think — "they" being an amorphous entity composed of France, Britain, and the United States. In other words, our friends, the good guys, who in my youthful fantasy were certainly already on their way to kidnap Hitler and lock him up and out of harm's way for the remainder of his life.

I was not consciously patriotic. My schoolmates and I sang the national anthem on appropriate occasions. We cheered loudly when the Dutch national soccer team scored a goal against Belgium, its archrival; we rejoiced in our queen's birthday because it meant a school holiday and a festive parade downtown. But I did not wholeheartedly share in the nation's joy at the wedding of Crown Princess Juliana and Bernhard, a German prince. Being German, he did not get my blessing.

At school, our geography lessons consisted of memorizing the names of the towns, rivers, and lakes of the Netherlands as well as of the islands, cities, and volcanoes of the Dutch colonies in the East and West Indies. In history class, we learned how the Dutch had pluckily fought off the invaders from mighty Spain, England, and France, and how the colonies had been won. Yet none of these events — neither the beginnings, the progress, nor the endings of our wars — was presented in a particularly stirring way. We were not aroused to feel any great passion for our homeland. We simply took for granted the cozy, nest-like atmosphere in which we lived.

Nor did I feel particularly Jewish. We were "Yom Kippur" Jews. My vague awareness of being a Jew came about through a special ritual, which had nothing to do with religion, to which I was treated on the first Sunday of each month. While other Jewish preteen boys attended Hebrew school, Father would take me on a tram ride to the Jewish quarter. On these Sunday mornings with Father, I was exempted from dressing up to please Mother. Wearing old plus fours, we would first stop at a bakery in the Jodenbreestraat, the main thoroughfare of Amsterdam's traditional Jewish neighborhood, for challah and ginger bolus, a traditional, strongly spiced Jewish cake. Then we would walk to visit Opoe and Omoe, Father's parents, who lived in a walk-up cold-water flat on the Rechtboomsloot, a canal in the old Jewish quarter. Besides the bread and ginger bolus, we also dropped off half a dozen oranges, a large piece of crumbling aged Gouda, and a bag of freshly roasted peanuts in the shell.

I liked to climb into Omoe's built-in bedstead on the

far wall of my grandparents' living room, close its shutters, and peek through its wooden slats at Father seated between his parents. Opoe was a shy and taciturn man who became eloquent when Father was his sole audience. At birthday celebrations, surrounded by his daughters with their husbands and children — and Father, Mother, and me — he would hardly utter a word.

Opoe was a diamond polisher by profession and a devoted member of his union. On our Sunday-morning visits he would report on the latest labor meeting or the May Day parade in which he had taken part: these were momentous occasions in his life. May Day was the most important day of the year, and he would repeat to us the rousing speeches he had heard, word by word. His union, he believed, would remedy the many grievances he and his coworkers held against the owners of the diamond factories.

Opoe never kissed me like Mother's dad, my other grandfather. But he always shook my hand when we parted. It made me feel grown-up, especially since I had been listening attentively from behind the shutters. It also made me proud, as if through his handshake I had been drawn into his circle.

Afterward, Father would take me by the hand, his other hand now holding the bag, which was now only half full. We would stroll through streets and alleys where Amsterdam's Jewish inhabitants clustered around their cavernous synagogues and scraped together a living as small shopkeepers, tailors, manufacturers of textiles and linens, clock makers, diamond polishers, and craftsmen in half a dozen other trades. Many were poor, and peddlers out of need. It was the only trade open to them.

Amsterdam had always prided itself on being an open and tolerant society — more so than any other European city. The niche that the Jews had carved out for themselves in Amsterdam was replenished by a continuous stream of new arrivals from Eastern Europe, replacing those who migrated to new middle-class neighborhoods, just a short tram ride away.

When Father married, he left the Jewish quarter for good. Mother's parents had moved out earlier; my maternal grandfather had prospered modestly from trading as a wholesaler of household goods.

My parents' generation was the first to fan out to new neighborhoods in significant numbers. They settled mainly to the south of Amsterdam's center. In the 1920s and 1930s the Jewish population of Amsterdam had swelled to 80,000, constituting well over half of all the Jews in Holland. It was one of the oldest and largest Jewish population centers in Western Europe. After World War II, about 5,000 Jews were left.

Where Father and I walked, Jews had lived since the sixteenth century. Rembrandt had lived and worked in this neighborhood, finding models among the archetypal patriarchs on his block.

As we strolled along the clothing and junk stalls at the

nearby Waterlooplein, Father firmly held my hand and told me not to touch. I needed Father's reassuring grip, as I was a little scared to be in a crowd of so many tall strangers wearing dark large-brimmed hats. On one special Sunday, a few days before Mother's birthday, Father selected a glittering brooch at a jewelry stall. It made Mother very happy.

By one o'clock we were home for our Sunday lunch. I would devour the open-face sandwiches — thick slices of heavily buttered challah with chunks of the sharp cheese on top. I would have ended up with a serious case of indigestion had Mother not called a halt to my gluttony. Even so, she let me crack a few peanuts — another special Sunday treat.

The rest of the peanuts were shared with my friends on our free Wednesday afternoons. We used to get together in a tent pitched on a sandy building site at the end of my street. First, we played Cowboys and Indians, ending our games with the peanut ritual. This consisted of our counting how many nuts were enclosed in each shell, and sorting the singles, doubles, and triples into separate heaps. The champion was entitled to eat as many of his winnings as he could stomach; the losers shared the rest.

In 1933, the year Hitler came to power, we moved to Scheveningen, a fishing village bordering The Hague. We lived in a cozy semidetached home in a prosperous middle-class neighborhood, opposite some tennis courts and close to a well-laid-out woodland park and one of Holland's widest, longest, and most endlessly overcrowded beaches. I was fifteen in the autumn of 1938, and remember having a strong sense of foreboding that mushroomed into fury and disgust when I watched my family react with relief and joy to the news coming out of the conference in Munich between Britain's Neville Chamberlain and Chancellor Hitler, at which the fate of Czechoslovakia was sealed.

We were all seated around the radio in the living room of my favorite aunt, Tante Aal, listening to the thunderous applause with which Chamberlain was welcomed back to London. Tante Aal, who was childless and lived on the same street as two of her sisters, was always well prepared for our family gatherings. Her table was invariably laden with chocolate-glazed cream puffs, chocolate cakes, truffles, nougat, and liqueur-filled bonbons.

Was the whole world ready to approve this sellout? Here was my own family cheering on old stuffed shirt Neville so that they, in their simplemindedness, could continue to put their trust in an ever-lasting peace! Only Father caught my eye and nodded thoughtfully at me. I shared his fear, and he shared my anger. In that one moment I felt very close to him: we both were appalled. The others, unaware of our outrage, earnestly redirected their attention to the rich assortment of light and dark brown confections displayed on the table in front of them.

The next memorable announcement I remember hearing on the radio was Chamberlain's speech of September 3, 1939, when Britain declared war on Germany, two days after the Germans invaded Poland.

During the eight months that followed — the so-called Phony War — I had a taste of things to come in biology class, where our teacher, a fervent Dutch Nazi, tried to convert us to his cause. In this, he generally failed. But he did provide me and my friends an instructive insight into the obsessions and objectives of national socialism. A convinced Darwinist, Mr. Brouwer explained German national socialism as the inevitable consequence of the evolution of the species, which placed a Teutonic *Herrenvolk* at the apex of a pyramid of all the world's races. It was the first time that my debating skills were seriously tested. The trouble was that I always seemed to arrive at the perfect knockout rebuttal in my bed, half a day too late.

Mr. Brouwer found two disciples in our class: Robby and Karel. They were much better on the tennis court than I and also had more stamina as long-distance skaters, boasting about their tours along Holland's frozen canals and ditches. They were pleasant enough and neither ever uttered an anti-Semitic remark in my hearing, although they forcefully expressed their pro-German sympathies and did not have a good word to say about the British. Both then joined the Dutch Nazi contingent that was sent to the Russian front, and both were killed.

Despite the precarious political situation, Mother traveled to Paris to see the new fashions. I was more interested in following the news from the front than in studying. My friends and I also put more energy into persuading our parents to allow us to throw parties than in finishing our schoolwork. At those parties, I tried to dance cheek to cheek with the girls in our class and rarely managed to steal a kiss.

In the winter and early spring of 1940, I was engaged in a weekly correspondence with Marie-France, a girl I had met the previous summer in France. Mother had arranged for me to stay with a family in Lyon who were in the silk business and who, to supplement their income, looked after young foreigners. I was one of six boarders staying with Marie-France's family, all in need of improving our French language skills. Marie-France and I held hands, kissed, and fumbled. It was my first puppy love. At the end of my vacation she accompanied me to the train station. We got there an hour before my train's departure. We held each other close and stared deeply into each other's eyes. Even while thus preoccupied, I could not help but notice that the station was swarming with soldiers.

My friend Jules van Hessen (the brother of the woman who would become my wife) was more successful with the girls than most. At school he and I shared a desk. We also shared the arrogant attitude of sixteen-year-olds toward our teachers, whom we judged to be mediocre or inferior, and in the case of Mr. Brouwer, obnoxious. Jules's family used to live in the "Belgian quarter" of Scheveningen where we did, and when we were younger Jules and I had often biked together to and from school. When it was stormy out, as it often is in Holland, we would arrive at our destination out of breath and often drenched to the skin.

In early September 1939, a few days after the Nazis invaded Poland, I received my first letter from Marie-France. Each page was decorated around the edges with hand-drawn pictures of the French tricolor, its vertical red, white, and blue interlocked with the horizontally striped red, white, and blue of my own Dutch flag. "We are one against our common enemy," she wrote. Her patriotic fervor notwithstanding, I was smitten. It was the first time that my fantasies were focused on a real-life girl. We continued to write each other once a week. I received a last letter from Lyon in the early days of May 1940, just before the Germans launched their invasion of Holland and Belgium, leading to their military victory over France. We never reestablished contact, and she disappeared from my life.

May 10, 1940. I was jolted awake by a big bang: the first German bombs fell on a military barracks less than half a mile from our home. There had been no warning. For the first eight months of the war, the German army had remained motionless opposite a French-British force on the Maginot line in the northeastern corner of France. Nobody in Holland had expected that we would become involved. We only realized what had happened when we turned on the radio and heard that German troops had crossed the Dutch-German frontier. The announcer exhorted us to remain calm and to look out for spies and traitors. We knew all about those: in Norway only a month earlier, a local Nazi leader named Quisling had played a treacherous role in the German invasion of Norway. The term *quisling*, meaning a traitor who will stab his own people in the back, had already entered the Dutch language.

After listening to the radio, I went out into the street, where I could smell the smoke coming from the burning barracks. Despite the early hour, our gang was out in force: two neighbor boys, Hans and Jaap, my cousin Dick, and myself.

We were very excited. None of us had the slightest intention of going to school, or even of finding out whether school was open. We wanted to make ourselves useful. We were all convinced that the Germans would be thrown back by immediate, massive reinforcements that were to come in from Britain. We wanted to witness the arrival of our allies and saviors, and to see German aircraft being shot down by our own fliers and the RAF. We went into the dunes as self-appointed spotters of German aircraft and any German parachutists who might drop down on our turf.

Over the next few days, Scheveningen, my hometown, became an imaginary battleground. We did not see a single German soldier, but rumors abounded that they were close by. Tanks were supposed to have entered neighboring The Hague. Hearsay had it that street-to-street and door-to-door fighting was taking place just south of us. Everyone was on an emotional roller coaster. (After the war I learned what really happened in our area during those days in May. In the first night of the war, sixty Dutch soldiers were killed in the air attack on the barracks near our home. German parachutists had been dropped south and east of the city with orders to capture Queen Wilhelmina and the royal family as well as the entire cabinet. That attack had been foiled, and many Germans were taken prisoner and immediately transported to England. Overall, the Dutch air defense forces around The Hague succeeded in downing about one hundred German warplanes. At no small cost, however: every single Dutch plane was destroyed.)

While my parents and my friends' parents wrung their hands, my friends and I spent our last moments of carefree boyhood on the alert in the dunes. In all those four days, we only spotted and booed one or two German reconnaissance planes. We had reason to cheer only once, when, in the far distance, we spied what we thought might be a lone Dutch fighter plane.

The dunes had always been my favorite playground, where, every day after school, I used to walk my dog, an oversize boxer. In the early evening, six days a week, in summer and in winter, I would run along the sandy footpath at the skirting of the dunes to meet Mother's commuter train at the Pomp Station, a small, open-air platform where only half a dozen trains stopped each day. My boxer pulled me along — I had to tug him back on his leash. Our route ran parallel to the imposing wall of the Scheveningse Gevangenis (the Scheveningen prison). One prison guard didn't like my dog and would shout at me to keep the leash tight. My dog would snarl back. On cold and rainy nights the prison would loom dark and threatening. During the war the prison was to achieve great notoriety: the Germans filled it with prominent Dutch citizens — some as hostages, others as suspects or members of the Resistance.

By day three we knew that the Luftwaffe had destroyed our airfields, but surely, we thought, the British and French would soon be on their way to save us, and would push back the Nazis before they could reach Amsterdam, The Hague, and the western part of the country. Our confidence in an imminent victory was bolstered by the news that our army engineers had breached the dikes, flooding the countryside. Making the roads impassable was easily accomplished, since much of the land in western Holland lies below sea level. It was a tactic rich in tradition: after all, breaching the dikes had stopped invaders in the past, including the Spaniards in the early 1600s and Louis XIV later in the same century. We were certain the German tanks would never make it this far.

The reality of our situation was driven home to us in the afternoon of May 14, when the announcement came over the radio: the Dutch army had capitulated. The Luft-waffe had pulverized neighboring Rotterdam, Holland's second-largest city and our most important harbor. To make matters worse, the queen and her family had fled to England, devastating our morale.

2

Escape

In my own family, major world events always seemed to find us seated around Tante Aal's table, heaped with cakes and pastries. I was slumped next to Dick, my eighteen-year-old cousin. There, on our day of shame and sadness, we hung our heads and blew our noses along with all the rest of our compatriots: 7 million people coming to terms with the awful truth — that the peaceful life we had known as a nation was over. Our life would now be directed by a hated enemy. We had no idea what he might do, but we feared the worst.

A strained voice on the radio announced that some units were continuing to resist in Zeeland, a province in the southwest of the country, bordering Belgium. Dick and I, eager for action, pushed our chairs back from the table and got to our feet. I announced that we were going down there to join the fighting. I remember the stricken look on the faces around that table, all of them too preoccupied with their own fears to react to what I was saying. None of us realized at that moment that we had just finished our last supper on native soil.

Grabbing our bicycles, Dick and I raced to the harbor of Scheveningen, a twenty-minute ride. Since the Germans had occupied most of the country, the logical road to Zeeland was by boat, heading south along the coast.

When we reached the harbor, we noticed scores of people huddled in clusters on the quays, gesticulating excitedly. Some were running from group to group. Serious negotiations were in progress. Huge sums of Dutch guilders, Swiss francs, and American dollars were being offered to any Scheveningen fisherman prepared to leave his family behind to ferry the prospective refugees across the North Sea to England.

Dick and I looked at each other. Going to England and volunteering over there seemed a much better plan than throwing in our lot with the remains of a defeated army. I saw a boy of around twelve, who was just standing there. I signaled him to come over.

"If you'll deliver this message for me," I said, "you can keep the bike." I quickly wrote my aunt's address on a piece of paper, folded it, and scribbled on the inside: "Dick and I are on our way to England. We are at the harbor. *Tot ziens* [Good-bye for now]."

The boy took the note and jumped on my bike. "He'll never deliver it," Dick muttered. We were standing close to one of the groups huddled there on the quay. I tried to wedge my way in even closer so I could overhear what they were saying. Surrounded by a protective wall of women and children, two middle-aged men were trying to strike a deal with a fisherman by showing him the contents of their open wallets. The fisherman was shaking his head.

I turned away and noticed four young men in their early twenties. They had been observing my transaction with the boy and the bike. Now they motioned us over. One said, "There's a lifeboat in the second harbor — over there. A big motorboat. We're going to see if we can take it to England. Want to come along?"

We jumped at the chance. I felt flattered to be asked. In the chaos of that hour, the kinship these young men felt for us — two high school kids who shared their determination to get over to England and fight the Germans — prompted them to include us in their group. It was a lucky break.

Three of our new companions were engineering students at Delft University, one of Europe's most prestigious technical and scientific academic institutions. The fourth, also a student, had cycled down from Groningen in the north, hoping to enlist in the army. We ran over to the second harbor, and there in front of us was a gleaming, new-looking lifeboat, property of Holland's volunteer coast guard. Its name — *Zeemans Hoop* (Seaman's Hope) — seemed a good omen.

A stocky man, the lone guard, was standing in the prow. As politely as possible, we asked him if he would please, please, take us to England.

"Over my dead body." He scowled. "Why don't you all get lost!"

Nobody moved. We remained where we were. He watched us warily, and we stared back at him. Nobody spoke. Then after a minute or two, to my utter amazement, he suddenly backed down. "All right, then," he said. "Take good care of her. And good luck. Watch out for those mines." He jumped ashore and walked away.

The boat was ours.

A crowd of people had spotted us and come running in our direction — men and women of all ages, including children, all waving and shouting that they wanted to be let on board. After we managed to let down the gangplank, the boat was filled in no time at all. Many of the people were carrying suitcases. All were well dressed: the men in suits, white shirts, and ties, the women in suits and high-necked blouses. All wore or carried over their arms a beige or navy blue raincoat — in 1940 casual clothes were not yet in fashion. Many of them spoke German. These were Jewish refugees from Germany, on the run once again.

One of the men who came aboard was a Dutch sergeant in uniform, armed with a rifle. He had deserted that afternoon when his unit had been ordered to surrender.

He made himself useful by firing over the heads of the crowd on the dock, because the boat was now full and the people left onshore were getting increasingly desperate. We were packed tight. "No more room," we shouted. "Sorry!" We started to cast off.

At that moment, a taxi drew right up to where the boat was tied up. I'll never know what compelled the driver to pull up to that particular spot. Out stepped Father, Mother, Tante Aal, and her husband, Max. And Dick's parents, Ro and John.

"No room," said one of the students.

"Can't you see we're full?" shouted another.

"But it's our parents!" Dick and I yelled.

Our family was allowed on board, and the gangplank was finally hauled in. Father quickly filled me in on what had happened. Contrary to Dick's expectations, the boy I'd given my bike to had kept his word. After he had delivered my note, Mother had shown no hesitation. She had stood up and declared: "Where my son goes, I go too." Wasting no time, the other members of the family had grabbed their suitcases and said that where Mother went, they would go too. On an impulse, driven by fear, three well-settled, middle-class couples left behind their homes, pets, carpets, family silver, stamp collections, furniture, and almost all of their wardrobes.

I was proud of Mother's display of reckless courage. I was not particularly surprised that the rest of family would follow her, even though I had never known them to be impulsive. Mother had a forceful personality. At the same time, I couldn't help feeling annoyed that just as I was about to embark on the first big adventure of my life, my entire family was there to share in, if not direct, my destiny.

Suddenly there was a commotion around the cabin in the middle of our boat. The motor would not turn over! While our sergeant discouraged several people onshore from trying to jump aboard our boat by threatening them with his rifle, our Delft engineering students frantically tried to start the motor. Finally they threw up their hands. They could not get it started.

The ploy of the gift of a bike was repeated, and a boy rode off to locate a member of the lifeboat's crew. He was back in no time with the boat's engineer, who lived nearby. He started the engine and was offered a small fortune to remain onboard, but he declined. Reluctantly, we dropped him off at the end of one of the two piers jutting out into a perfectly calm sea.

"Watch out for mines!" he warned from the shore.

A roll call was taken, and each passenger's name was recorded in a log. The tally was forty-six people, most of whom looked anxious and scared. Only our group of high school and college students, proud of our success so far, kept up a show of bravado.

Only years later did I learn that, except for one small sailboat, the *Zeemans Hoop* was the only refugee boat to make it out of the harbor of Scheveningen that night.

There were two doctors aboard. An inventory revealed a limited amount of drinking water, half a dozen bottles of rum stashed away for emergencies on those stormy winter nights when the crew of the *Zeemans Hoop* performed its regular lifesaving duties, a number of first aid kits, and a dozen or so chocolate bars, which one of the parents had prudently packed to keep his child quiet.

I was assigned to be a forward lookout for mines. From the newsreels, I was familiar with what a mine looked like — a barrel-shaped form floating in the water. Night was falling. It was a glorious evening, clear and calm. Standing in the prow, scanning the water, I didn't dare to turn around to watch the distant spectacle of the city of Rotterdam going up in smoke, the result of the massive German air raid. I listened to the exclamations of my travel companions as they described the scene — a red, glowing blaze veiled in black smoke, gradually fading into the night.

Focused on my mine-detecting responsibility, I was too excited to consider what must be going through the minds of my parents and the other older passengers who had left behind their friends, their relatives, their homes, and all their worldly possessions. Now we — the Dutch, who had thought it impossible that our country would ever be occupied by an enemy — were on the run. Now we too were refugees.

We were still within sight of land when our engine coughed and died. The *Zeemans Hoop* lay still in the water.

Gentle waves lapped at the sides of the boat, the edge of our existence. The sky was bright and starlit. I wondered where the seagulls had gone.

A man with a double-barreled name and the title "Jonkheer," signifying membership in the Dutch nobility, started bellowing at the top of his voice, demanding that we return to port — "for the sake of the women and children." Others joined in. But the rest argued equally loudly that it would be dangerous to turn back, since there was no way of knowing what the German occupiers would do to us.

It started as a sort of open debate. Then the argument got ugly. Although we had little room to move about, someone shoved somebody else. Cries of "Look out!" and "Be careful!" rang out. A line was drawn between some of the older generation (though not the members of my family) who wanted to return, and the young, who insisted on going on. There was also contempt for the Jonkheer, whose very name, title, and accent aroused feelings of class antagonism. When I realized that what we were talking about involved the risk of our being arrested by the Gestapo, I began to shake. This was serious business — our very survival was at stake. My flight had been launched head-over-heels in a spirit of adventure; I had had no time to consider the consequences. Now that we were stuck dead in the water, reality set in. I must say something, I thought. I have to find an irrefutable argument that will clinch it once and for all and convince all aboard that there is no choice but to go on. But once again my throat was dry, and I clammed up, just as I used to in Mr. Brouwer's natural history class. In order to speak up, I had to overcome the respect for my elders that had been drummed into me since childhood. I just couldn't do it.

The debate was now really getting out of hand. People were shrieking and yelling and interrupting each other. And then suddenly the discussion came to an abrupt stop. An eerie silence followed. It was as if it had suddenly hit every passenger aboard that here we were, drifting helplessly at sea. What had we done? What was next? Everyone in that lifeboat seemed to have been struck dumb. Perhaps we were waiting for one person to come forward and be decisive, to show some leadership. Then a lone voice, timid and hesitant, suggested a vote. That hardly made sense to me either: democracy at work in an open vessel on the high seas? Before the polling could start, however, one of the students finally took charge. All those who were having second thoughts, he yelled, should simply swim back to shore. The mutiny subsided as quickly as it had begun.

Meanwhile, two of the other student engineers had been tinkering with the motor below deck. After what seemed like hours but must have been less than fifteen minutes, they succeeded in getting it started again. Our voyage was resumed, and we chugged along at the same steady pace as before. The four students were still firmly in command. Families sat huddled together on the benches along both sides of the *Zeemans Hoop*. Everyone was quiet, looking back at Holland's disappearing coastline. Only the children slept.

At daybreak a formation of bombers flew over us. We assumed they were German, though they were too high for us to gauge whether they were friend or foe. An elderly couple told the sergeant he had better hide his rifle under his coat; if he didn't, we might be mistaken for a military target. The unidentified aircraft ignored us. They were undoubtedly after bigger game.

The sun rose in a breathtaking pink dawn. "Another beautiful day," we said to one another. Except for the children, no one complained of hunger or thirst; we were too scared, too excited, or both. After mistakenly identifying a large piece of driftwood as a mine, I finally spotted a barrel-like object that looked as if it might be the real thing. We gave it a wide berth.

It was midafternoon when two large shadows suddenly loomed up on the horizon. In the bright sunlight we could not make out what they were — only that they were rapidly closing in on us. Few of us had ever lived through so many hair-raising events in such a short space of time — first the motor dying within sight of land, then the bombers overhead, then the mine. As for me, it was all only part of a great adventure.

Whatever it was that was heading toward us was moving with great speed. The quick succession of so many panicky moods, so many ups and downs, was my initiation into the sort of spontaneous mass hysteria which I found myself part of several times in my life. After the passage of so many years, I cannot recall how, as a teenager, I coped with a number of crises that so quickly succeeded one another. I must have been uplifted when one euphoric moment followed the other and depressed when such glimpses of hope and relief were quickly overtaken by new calamities.

As the lead ship came closer, a cheer went up. She was flying the Union Jack! She was a destroyer: the *HMS Venomous* — a name meant to strike fear into the enemy, but one that, to us, meant we were safe at last. Soon we were alongside. A rope ladder was lowered, and British sailors helped us climb aboard — women and children first. The women squealed as the sailors lifted them up onto the deck. Everybody was laughing, though there were also copious tears of relief. We were formally welcomed onto English soil and invited to partake in high tea.

An announcement came over the public address system: the captain was inviting the crew of the *Zeemans Hoop* to join him on the bridge. Dick and I tagged along with the four students, who were the true heroes of the day. Up on the bridge, the captain showed us charts of the sea we had just crossed, pointing out several minefields strung just below the surface of the water. We had passed right over them, oblivious to the danger. It was only thanks to our unusually shallow draft that our boat had not been blown to pieces.

He also told us that our navigation skills left something

to be desired. The North Sea currents had driven us south toward the British Channel. Had we continued on our course, we would have missed the English coast altogether and been swept into the Atlantic Ocean, headed for the American continent. We stared at the captain with a mixture of relief and utter disbelief.

It wasn't until half a century later that I learned the full extent of our luck that day. In the German naval archives there is a report by the captain of a German U-boat, who writes that on May 15, 1940, he had the *HMS Venomous* in sight through his periscope just as a group of civilians were being taken on board. We owed our survival to the fact that both his submarine and a second U-boat that was also in the area had used up their supply of torpedoes on an earlier mission.

In The Hague, my parents had had the foresight to pack a small suitcase for each of us, containing some clothes, a toothbrush, and other essentials. Father's also contained most of our savings, in the form of bearer bonds that he had retrieved from his bank's safe deposit box. Once aboard the destroyer, Father discovered that, in the haste and confusion of departure, he had picked up the wrong suitcase. The one Mother had been watching like a hawk throughout our voyage turned out to be filled not with bonds but with clothes hangers! Fortunately, Father had stuffed some valuables in his pockets, and Mother had some large banknotes in various currencies and gold coins in her handbag. We were not entirely destitute.

We also had our passports. In Dover, where we dis-embarked, the British authorities processed us quickly. We were served tea, first by the immigration people and again on the platform of the rail station, by a group of kind ladies who belonged to a volunteer organization. A couple of hours later we boarded a train for London.

3

Refuge

As SOON AS WE ARRIVED IN ENGLAND, it became clear that my ambition to join up had been unrealistic. There was as yet no organized Dutch army. When I walked into a British recruiting office, I was told in no uncertain terms that I was too young to enlist in any military force.

We lived four months in London, our home a small hotel off Russell Square. Dutch refugees occupied most of the rooms in our hotel. When I wasn't called to accompany my parents, I hung around the lobby, playing bridge or chess and flirting with the pretty switchboard operator. I also explored the neighborhood and visited some of London's tourist attractions, but for the most part I was bored. The only exciting distractions consisted of the occasional dash to the air raid shelter and my attempts to impress the receptionist, who paid not the slightest attention. I was itching for new adventure.

A week or two after arriving, my parents visited Mother's London business contacts. Some of these were Jewish refugees from Germany, who had lost no time reestablishing themselves in a new country. I went along, serving as translator, because Father knew no English, while Mother managed to make herself understood by mixing a few vaguely English-sounding words into her heavily Dutch-accented German and accompanying this mélange with energetic gestures. Although she did usually manage to get across her message — that we had left home and worldly possessions behind — she came away from her conversations with only the faintest notion of what the other person had said in reply.

Mother's friends had built up their new businesses in England in the trade they had left behind, which was ladies' millinery. We must have visited one contact a day over a three-week period. Each milliner referred us to the next one. I dreaded those visits; they were a terror for me. I was always complimented on my English and sometimes patted on the head. But I was deeply embarrassed when these silver-haired, elegantly dressed, and heavily accented gentlemen would press a small bundle of pound notes into Mother's hands. As Mother dabbed at her eyes, I would look away, furious, ashamed, and humiliated. At those moments I resented my mother even more than I had when she forced me to wear a sailor suit or fancy plus fours.

My own English was rather good. At school, English had been my favorite subject. From the age of twelve I had listened to the BBC, marveling at the wit of Noel Coward and the deadpan presentation of the six o'clock news. In 1938 I spent a long summer holiday in Dorset. A voracious reader, I had devoured more books in English than in Dutch. Charles Dickens, Sir Walter Scott, Oscar Wilde, and J. B. Priestley were among my literary heroes. I loved the *New Statesman*, Agatha Christie, and the *London Illustrated News*. In London I continued to tune in to the BBC breathlessly, following the course of the war. (After the war I learned that our *Zeemans Hoop* had been put to good use by the British: it had made several trips to evacuate British troops from Dunkirk.)

While Mother made her rounds, Father had absolutely nothing to do. Yet he looked more preoccupied and worried than I had ever seen him before. He put a damper on my optimism by sharing his concern with me over the rapid victory the German armies had scored in France, which, he was certain, would be followed by an invasion and the inevitable German conquest of England. Although I could not imagine such a disaster, I felt helplessly small trying to argue with my own father.

One day a fellow refugee in our hotel asked whether I would like to learn the diamond trade. I was curious about the offer but loath to accept it. Father urged me to give it a try, and Mother was determined to get me out of our hotel's lobby, where I was wasting my time making eyes at the receptionist. After thinking about how bored I was, I reconsidered. A day later I was an apprentice in the diamond trade. All the action took place in just one street — Hatton Garden — where transactions were conducted in the open air. I followed my tutor around for a few days, watching as small envelopes containing half a dozen or a dozen stones were passed from hand to hand, the gems studied through a loupe and appraised for value. Bids were made, rejected, increased, and finally accepted. Each trader made a modest profit on every transaction, but at the end of the day I wondered what the point was. It seemed to me that the merchandise had merely been recycled. Within a week, I told my parents that this kind of apprenticeship was a waste of time as far as I was concerned. I found the entire business useless and embarrassing. Both Father and Mother told me how disappointed they were, but they weren't able to change my mind.

It struck me how separate the circles were in which I now moved. There were the relatives and the members of my new extended family from the *Zeemans Hoop*. They were the protective core around me; a very familiar environment, no matter how displaced we all were. Compared with this Dutch coterie, Mother's milliner benefactors were aliens: they spoke German among themselves, and their English was heavily accented. The English receptionists and other hotel staff members eyed us warily, sometimes making us feel like intruders, while the diamond traders in Hatton Garden seemed to come from a different planet. The last group I was dealing with, the Dutch government bureaucrats-in-exile, also seemed to operate on a unique island of their own. They maintained a stiff and formal attitude toward us, the humble subjects of Her Royal Highness. I started to wonder how everyone could be so preoccupied with his or her own little world; was there anything that tied us all together? I knew that there were Belgian and French refugees close by. I never met a single one. There was a war going on out there, but we had secured a little niche; I moved about quite comfortably and contentedly in the small cocoon that our family had built for itself.

My parents were not the only ones concerned about my future: no less a personage than the Dutch minister of waterworks, Mr. Alberda, who had been a neighbor of ours in Scheveningen, took an interest in me. His ministry had overseen the building and maintenance of water projects — Holland's extensive network of drainage canals and protective dikes, a very important matter in a country that lies largely below sea level. Exiled in London with the rest of the cabinet, he now seemed to have all the time in the world to take a young neighbor's case to heart.

His suggestion was that I should finish my schooling in the Dutch East Indies. That archipelago (today the Republic of Indonesia) beckoned as an attractive destination. Mother had a cosmopolitan outlook, the result of years of buying trips to Paris, London, and Vienna, and she immediately saw the move as an opportunity. Father, who generally let Mother call the shots, agreed that the prospect of a new life in the Orient, far from the war in Europe, looked good. He had just one reservation: it was supposed to be uncomfortably hot out there, and he feared Mother might suffer from the heat. However, convinced that the war would not be over soon, he saw no point in hanging around London waiting for the day when we could return home.

Meanwhile, Mr. Alberda had arranged a meeting with one of his colleagues, the now similarly underemployed minister of justice. Professor Gerbrandy, who sported a thick walrus mustache, agreed with the plan and authorized a government loan for our passage. He even promised me that, upon finishing high school on Java, I could return to Europe to fight the Germans — although, he added, he could not guarantee that the war would last that long. There was every reason to believe that the Germans would be defeated long before I graduated in 1941. (Gerbrandy, who was subsequently promoted to Prime Minister in exile, maintained his staunchly optimistic outlook throughout the war.)

Our family was offered passage on a Cunard ocean liner. Our final destination was Batavia (now Jakarta), capital of Holland's crown colony, at the farthest remove — or so we thought — from the war.

Our last meal in London with the whole family was a tearful occasion. Tante Aal and her husband Max had decided to stay behind in England. Max had found a job as a diamond polisher in Llandudno, Wales. But Aunt Ro, Uncle John, and Cousin Dick threw their lot in with us. Mother and her sisters were very close. All through dinner, the tears flowed freely. "We'll be safe over there," said Uncle John. "The Japanese will never enter a war they cannot win." It surprised me that Father did not say a word, but I was so preoccupied with my own feelings that I did not ask him what he was thinking.

On a dreary day in early September, we boarded a train to Liverpool, where our ship was docked. The *Viceroy of India*, bound for Singapore, was one of four large ocean liners that had been converted into troop carriers and that would be traveling in convoy.

That first night at sea, my thoughts went back to our earlier voyage, on the *Zeemans Hoop*. This time I felt much more secure. Snug in my cabin, seeing the ships signaling to each other in the dark — a series of single, blinding lights transmitting mysterious coded messages — I felt safe. But by the following day the other three ships were gone — on their way to America, we were told. The fact that we were now unescorted and alone made Mother and many others aboard anxious.

Because the Mediterranean was a war zone, the Suez Canal was closed to us. Instead, we had to go around the Horn of Africa. Our voyage lasted seven mostly uneventful weeks under an often burning equatorial sun. Dick and I struck up a friendship with the two Royal Air Force sergeants who shared our cabin. They kept us apprised of how far they had gone — or had been allowed to go — in their nightly trysts with two British army nurses also en route to the Far East. The morning-after instruction about the correct use of the condom (which they called a French letter) and other clinical details fascinated me. Our roommates were only three years older than we, but their experience was light-years ahead of ours. In any event, their reports of sexual prowess kept me awake at night, feverishly wondering how much longer I was doomed to remain a virgin.

I also formed a friendship with two Dutch Jesuit priests, who provided me with a different kind of instruction. Every morning at ten I would accompany them on a brisk walk along the deck. They had been attending a meeting of their order in England at the time of the German invasion of Holland and, like us, were now refugees on their way to the Indies to assume new teaching assignments. I have only a dim memory of the younger one, a hearty, rotund figure. By contrast, I have a vivid recollection of the older priest's long nose and strong jaw, and of our struggle to keep our daily conversation audible — walking around the deck against the wind or with a gale at our backs. The priest was punctilious in his use of language. His lecturing left little room for dialogue, although I usually managed to get a few questions in. His subject was the Dutch war of liberation from Spain in the sixteenth and seventeenth centuries. He seldom talked about his religious beliefs, and rarely related them to that early war when the Protestant Dutch fought Catholic Spain. My friend extolled the virtues of the Dutchman's national self-determination and glossed over any reference to the dogmas of his own church, which had been largely responsible for the Dutch insurrection against Spanish rule and had turned the Dutch into fervent iconoclasts. He did, however, draw analogies between the past and our country's current plight, reinforcing my own conviction that the Germans were going to lose, even if they seemed invincible now. His encyclopedic knowledge excited me: he spouted facts, anecdotes, and insights. These conversations stimulated a passion for history that has never left me.

One day, off the coast of West Africa, our ship suddenly made an abrupt about-turn. Standing on deck, squinting into the glaring sun, we could not make out what was going on until we pulled up alongside a smaller ship, a freighter. When we saw the rope ladders hanging over its side and a flotilla of lifeboats bobbing in the ocean below, we understood what was going on. Soon our ship, too, was engaged in pulling sailors aboard. It was the crew of a British merchant vessel that had been sunk by a German battleship — the notorious *Graf Spee*.

Later I listened as one of the shipwrecked men recounted how his vessel had been overtaken by a magnificent apparition moving at dazzling speed; how the crew had been allowed five minutes to lower and board their lifeboats; how a single German torpedo had efficiently dispatched his ship to her watery grave; and how the *Graf Spee* had then vanished as swiftly and stealthily as she had appeared.

Capetown was our first port of call. My RAF friends

and I visited a bar swarming with Allied soldiers, sailors, and airmen dressed in all shades of khaki, navy, green, and white. The British were on their way to the Far East, while the Australians and New Zealanders were headed for England. We drank beer, and then some more beer. The inevitable brawl broke out — my first. I would have expected it to be a fight either between visitors and locals or between different branches of the armed forces, but to my surprise, it turned out to be a confrontation between those age-old antagonists — the English and the Irish. My RAF friends tried to melt away unnoticed. I did not want to get involved in the scuffle either. I succeeded in making a getaway through a back alley when the MPs arrived to arrest the bloodied combatants.

Back on board, my parents were waiting for me. Mother was fuming. To punish me for going to a bar and staying out late, they forbade me to go ashore again. Luckily for me, our ship sailed the next morning, and by the time we reached Durban, on the east coast of South Africa, our next port of call, the whole incident had been forgotten. Mother, deprived of her work, her home, her circle of friends, doted on me more than ever. I felt she was watching me like a hawk. She meant to discipline me, but she always ended up forgiving me. The most I ever got was a severe talking-to, which I tended to ignore or soon forgot.

I was still a news junkie. Once a day the British troops were informed how the war was progressing. I always sidled up to the crowd of soldiers seated on the main deck as they were briefed about what was going on back home. The German air assault on Britain had started in earnest. An enthusiastic cheer went up from the deck when the German aircraft losses were announced. I don't recall any mention of developments in Asia or anywhere else in the world. The British soldiers' interest was focused on events affecting the families they had just left behind. My shipmates were on their way to the colonies in Singapore or Malaya or Borneo to strengthen the British regiments already there. They had been sent to reinforce the already considerable power of the British Empire in Southeast Asia, not as a warning to Japan but simply as an additional insurance policy. No one thought that Japan would ever dare attack the British lion. (Little did my fellow passengers or I know what was in store for us.)

There were two more brief shore visits: Mombasa, Kenya, and Bombay. Bombay was our first encounter with the East. My parents were appalled by the squalor. I found the teeming crowds of people, the temples, the mosques, the smells, and the tastes wildly exciting. We walked through the bazaar, where I saw British soldiers and white women buy foods and haggle over scarves, ornamental swords, and silver trinkets. I experimented: biting into snacks and fruits that I had never seen before, despite Mother's strong signs of disapproval. It was overwhelming; I felt that the Orient would bewitch me.

After one more week at sea, I said good-bye to my British friends in Singapore. Our family transferred to a

Dutch steamer, which took us to Batavia. Compared to Bombay, Batavia was very clean and orderly. We rented a large white villa on a fastidiously neat Dutch street. It could have been Holland, except for the tropical plants and trees, the lizards on the wall of my bedroom, and the monkeys in the backyard. Mother soon found a job as manager of the local branch of Gerzon, a Dutch fashion store chain. (Her predecessor had been on home leave when war broke out in Holland and was now trapped there.) Father and Uncle John began to import dresses from the United States, which were sold to retail stores throughout the islands. Our financial house was back in order in no time.

Mother was, as Father had feared, greatly bothered by the tropical heat, despite which she threw herself wholeheartedly into her work. Back in Holland, she had loved socializing with her colleagues, the other buyers at the Bijenkorf department store, where she had spent most of her adult life. In Batavia, she was the boss, and she found that bosses have few friends. She felt lonely and clung to me more tenaciously than ever. My resistance to her grew, and I tried to evade her attentions as often as I could. At age seventeen, I couldn't tolerate her great motherly love. I felt closer to Father, with whom I would discuss the political and military news every day after we finished reading the local papers. I also respected Father's knowledge of Italian opera and his love for Enrico Caruso and Beniamino Gigli, whereas I looked down on Mother's favorites — the operettas of Johann Strauss and Franz Lehar and the tenor Richard Tauber.

An outstanding bridge player, Father had starred in bridge tournaments back home. Now in our high-ceilinged, fan-cooled living room in Jakarta, he helped me solve bid and finesse problems laid out in a book by Ely Culbertson, one of his heroes.

Like most colonial families, we had four servants: a cook, a laundress, a gardener, and a *djongos* (boy). The *djongos* was married to our cook and fulfilled many functions — major domo, waiter, valet, handyman, local guide, interpreter, and general factotum. I shared the general colonial indifference to the natives. I neither knew nor cared about what happened in the buildings at the back of the kitchen, where our staff lived. I only knew that they shared their quarters with an indeterminate number of relatives. We paid them the standard wage — a pittance by our standards, but which furnished them with all that they needed, or all we thought they needed. They seemed happy, content, and always cheerful. Occasionally, when I'd go to the back to look at the monkeys playfully throwing nuts at each other, the whole staff and their families would stand around me, watching with me, clapping and laughing.

My father and I, preoccupied with world events, paid little attention to what was going on locally. Father thought that the war in Europe would last many years, and he was also afraid that the Japanese might come down our way. We were not struck by the incongruity of our position as part of that small circle of Caucasians who lorded it over masses of indigenous people. We were *tuan* (sir) to the natives, whom we addressed indiscriminately as *djongos*. To the Indonesians we belonged to the ruling class; we were all members of the same white ghetto. As a matter of fact, we were outsiders ourselves: the highly hierarchal and undemocratic white society neither cared for, nor took an interest in, the small group of refugees from the home country. We did not belong to any of the rigorously established classes of privileged Dutchmen. Of the long-settled colonials, each had a specific role in the administration of indigenous Indonesian affairs. It was a highly organized structure. Each pillar of the colonial empire employed a set number of civil servants, military officers, teachers, planters, judges, and bankers, as well as a small number of businessmen who directed the monopolistic ownership of the archipelago's natural resources. As a salesman and a working woman, my parents did not fit into any acceptable category. Father never complained. Once he told me that he missed meeting his friends at eleven o'clock for a cup of coffee at Scheltema, a café in Amsterdam frequented by newspapermen and business people; "We could really talk there — we might agree or disagree, but we always respected each other's opinion." Whenever we went out, mingling with compatriots of my parents' generation, I realized that we were regarded as aliens.

It was different at school. Most of the teachers were Dutch, but the majority of my classmates — all except two Dutch boys and one girl — were either native Indonesian, Eurasians (*Indiesch*), or Chinese. I don't know now if my classmates saw things as I did, but it seemed to me that we were a well-integrated group, equals in every way. Even here, however, age-old strictures and taboos remained in force. There was camaraderie in the classroom and on the sports field, but visits to a friend's home were confined to classmates of one's own color.

One of my best friends was Hans, whose father was an officer in the navy. During the Easter school break of 1941, Hans and I went on a holiday camping trip in the mountains of eastern Java. On a high plateau, we were far away from the hustle and bustle of the overpopulated regions of the towns and valleys of western Java. Of course, we were accompanied by a watchful *djongos* who earned his keep by carrying our gear, putting up our tent, cooking our food, washing our clothes, and skillfully wielding a long bamboo stick to dispose of a very large cobra.

After passing my final high school exams in the spring of 1941, I worked for a couple of months for Borsumij (Borneo Sumatra Trading Company), a Dutch conglomerate with ownership interests in a number of shipping companies, plantations, and other major colonial enterprises. I was to be an apprentice trader once again, this time not in diamonds but in commodities. I was given basic instruction in the intricacies of selling my company's share of Indonesia's agricultural and mineral wealth on the world's markets.

Having grown up in Holland with the concept that the East Indies were an integral part of the Netherlands — for now and for all time — I was blissfully unconscious of the pomposity with which we Dutch comported ourselves; nor was I particularly bothered by the white man's discriminatory practices. I had not yet understood that we were hoarding, rather than sharing, our technical, agricultural, industrial, financial, and economic expertise and skills. Nor did I realize that among native Indonesians, only a privileged few were permitted to obtain an education beyond the elementary level.

Dressed in one of my white linen suits, which were washed and pressed daily by our laundress, I arrived at the office at seven and took my seat at a desk in the large trading room filled with managers, clerks, and other trainees. Preparing for the oppressive humidity that would soak us in a matter of hours, my colleagues and I would immediately take off our jackets, but an unwritten dress code forbade us to loosen our ties.

One fine day in the summer of 1941, my civilian status came to an end, and I was drafted into the Royal Dutch East Indian Army. I was happy to go. Little did I realize that I was moving from one rigid colonial system into another. From the day we had arrived in the Indies, Father and Mother had been apprehensive about the prospect of my military service. But the draft papers, giving me thirty days' notice, certainly did not come as a surprise. I had reached the age of eighteen, and this was, after all, wartime. I was billeted in the barracks of Bandung, a hill town in western Java, north of Batavia.

Bandung looked very much like a Dutch town, an unusually prosperous Dutch town at that. Even its center was peaceful and quiet compared to the hustle and bustle of metropolitan Batavia. Only the green lushness of the hilly landscape made it seem worlds apart from the flat, monotonous Dutch countryside I had left behind. On Sundays, bicycling back to the barracks after a game of bridge at a friend's house, I enjoyed the calm and pressure-free atmosphere that was a part of the spirit of the city and all its inhabitants, irrespective of race and color. The streets I biked through were not only tranquil and nearly free of traffic but as neat and clean as if the proverbial Dutch housewife had just attacked them with her broom.

Boot camp was not easy for me. I had never been particularly athletic. I had a hard time keeping up with my co-conscripts and was often the last to arrive at the finish when ordered to run on the double, scale a wall, jump a ditch, or surmount miscellaneous other obstacles. Our instructor was a veteran of the regular professional army who after more than ten years of service still had not managed to rise above the rank of corporal. In drill exercises he seemed to take pleasure in singling me out, berating me for the clumsiness with which I manipulated my rifle. The corporal had it in for me in many ways. He found me deficient in standing to attention and in responding to his other commands. He found fault with the way I wore my puttees and with my performance during morning exercises. "You laugh too much; you are too happy!" he yelled. Tattooed snakes, lions, and eagles protruded from the sleeves of his khaki shirt and stuck out below the rim of his army shorts. My friends and I had a good time speculating what other animals might be creeping around those parts of his body that were not exposed. "You no-good rich kid!" he yelled and made me pump and stretch out my right arm, with my rifle as ballast, a hundred times. It was a painful punishment, which I was often physically unable to complete. But I learned how to dramatize, exaggerating the discomfort. Since the corporal yelled all the time, his yelling did not particularly bother me — which infuriated him all the more.

The worst part of the training was when we had to crawl on our bellies under low-strung barbed wire. The mud was sticky and smelly, and the insects swarmed down on us and would not leave us alone. Each exercise lasted about an hour but was repeated again and again, from seven until noon. Promptly at twelve, we stopped. I had had it. I couldn't wait to get out of the rice paddy and run all the way back to the nearest shower. But my corporal often made me go back and repeat the entire exercise. I had been too slow, he said. Even that did not dampen my spirit; I felt invincible.

Most of my fellow recruits were Eurasians. I felt relaxed

in their company; we all enjoyed a great feeling of cama-raderie. In the barrack-room banter, I became one of the lead comics, cracking jokes, inventing funny new epithets and ever dirtier expressions. There was some teasing and a lot of sexual innuendo. We saved our most creative efforts for the curses aimed at our corporal.

Most of us had just graduated from high school. As such, we were slated to become officers. A few of my friends and I rebelled, however, refusing to go into officer training; any appeal the military life might have held for us had vanished during the first weeks of our induction into the army. But the hierarchal system was relentless. I was promoted despite myself. Soon I was made corporal, then sergeant. I took no particular pride in my new rank but was glad to be rid of my drill instructor.

If I had thought being stationed in Bandung would mean being rid of Mother, I was mistaken. She arranged for a room to be put at my disposal in the house of a col-league, the manager of the Bandung branch of Gerzon. The servants in that house took care of my laundry, pressed my uniform, and cooked a meal for me whenever I asked them to. If I had been permitted to take my rifle home, they would have cleaned that, too. As it was, one of the men in my barracks volunteered to do this for me, for a modest fee.

Every Saturday morning an envelope was left in my room, filled with a generous amount of cash. Mother's letters from Batavia arrived twice a week, and when I failed to respond to her urgent pleas to come home on weekends, she took the train and lay in wait for me at the gate to our barracks.

Saturday night was the big night out — but only when I could manage to escape Mother. Seated at the lively bar of Hotel Homann, Bandung's only luxury hotel, sipping Scotch and smoking Egyptian cigarettes, I imagined myself a sophisticated man of the world. In truth, however, I watched enviously as other young men, in and out of uniform, danced with attractive young women whose parents had allowed them to go out on a date. By the end of the evening, one or two similarly unattached young men usually joined me, and we would pass the time deep in political or philosophical discussion until the bar closed.

Refugees tend to seek each other out; the new social crowd my parents were drawn to was composed of other newly arrived refugees from Holland. On one of my visits home I met Betty, a tall, beautiful blond. Her parents had been the proprietors of a prosperous beauty salon in the heart of Amsterdam. I fell for her, head over heels. She allowed me one fleeting kiss and an awkward squeeze, but otherwise my advances were not encouraged. She would flirt over my shoulder with every other young man in the vicinity, which did little to improve my self-esteem. After returning to Bandung, I lost track of her. My short-lived infatuation left me feeling more sexually frustrated than ever.

After lights-out, our dormitory buzzed with whispered descriptions of sexual exploits. It was too hot and humid to put my head under the pillow. I was forced to listen to the boasts and fantasies of what seemed like an entire company of young Don Juans.

I hoped we would never have to meet an enemy. To me, our army seemed like a joke. We had just received new Canadian light and mobile antitank guns — weapons that were guaranteed to blow Japanese tanks to pieces. The trouble was that the gun sights were missing. They were nowhere to be found; we assumed they had been sent to another country, or unloaded on some faraway Indonesian island. Meanwhile, without the gun sights, the guns were useless. We could not take aim.

There also was a problem with our new two-way radio communications. For some unfathomable reason, these functioned pretty well only when two parties communicated at a very short distance — within earshot of each other. As for our army-issue boots, these came only in one, very large, size. Most of us had to stuff them with newspaper to make them fit, resulting in painful blisters and the indignity of ink-stained feet.

On December 7, 1941, the Japanese attacked Pearl Harbor. To us this news was eclipsed by the more direct threat to our region by the unexpected Japanese incursions in Southeast Asia. I saw a deadly threat in the swift southward advance of Japanese armies into Siam (Thailand), French Indochina (Vietnam), and Malaya (Malaysia), all occurring simultaneously. Clearly, this was all headed in our direction. I had a recurrent dream of escape, but how and where? I could desert, but Australia, India, and America were thousands of miles away, and the Japanese seemed to be everywhere else. I was trapped.

As the Japanese cycled down the Malay Peninsula toward Singapore, I did not hear any confidence-building messages coming from high up. Not a word was said about where and how our army might form a line of defense. The future did not seem very promising. I could not understand what my superiors were up to. For my part, I was convinced that one of Japan's primary motives for going to war was to pluck the rich pickings of the Indonesian archipelago, especially its oil and rubber. To me, Japan's occupation and our defeat were a foregone conclusion.

The closer the Japanese came, the more threatening they seemed. From general to private, we had all been conditioned to look down on the "Nip." We held to the Western image of the Japanese — sinister and strange. Their successes were therefore doubly alarming.

Our morale — not high to begin with — sank to its greatest depth. But we did start to take soldiering more seriously. Every other morning we were taken to the rifle range and competed as sharpshooters. Our weekend passes were canceled; Mother came to visit every Sunday, despite the long round-trip train journey from Jakarta to Bandung.

When Singapore fell, on February 15, 1942, I lost all respect for the British. I had counted on them to have better defenses than ours. For the first time, I decided not to entrust the cleaning of my weapon to anyone else. I polished my ancient and clumsy Lee Enfield rifle as if my life and the defense of our island depended on it.

Finally, March 1, 1942, came the moment of truth: Japanese forces invaded Java. We were confined to barracks, in a state of high alert. An enemy plane dropped a single load of bombs near our compound. Battalions and squadrons were marched from one end of our exercise field to the other, to no purpose that I could determine.

Our army panicked. We sent a mobile kitchen, complete with cooks and dishwashers, to spearhead one of our defense positions. Somehow the fighting units had managed to lag behind. For one day I waited nervously, praying that the rumors of valiant Dutch frontline troops halting the Japanese offensive would turn out to be true. Then I was ordered to go into battle.

Our orders were to go down a road along which the Japanese were expected to advance. We went in three trucks, each holding a sergeant, a corporal, and eighteen privates — sixty-odd adolescents in all, with hardly any combat training between us. In the first truck, a professional sergeant-major was in overall command. A lone soldier on a motorbike had been assigned to scout the terrain in front. For firepower, each truck counted one old-fashioned machine gun and our slow-loading rifles. We carried a small reserve of bullets in our belts. No one spoke.

I was in the last truck. The men, or boys, under my

command were Eurasian recruits. I had never met any of them before. We were all nervous. The scout returned to report that, up ahead, the road narrowed into a kind of tunnel, with high ridges on either side. If we went on, we could be sitting ducks for a Japanese ambush. But our sergeant-major was fearless. It was probably also his first armed engagement. He gave the sign to go forward. I launched into a military pep talk, exhorting my terrified troops to stay calm and hold their fire. That was the only strategy I could come up with. "Hold your fire." I said. "When we're all out of the truck and in the field, don't fire until I tell you."

As luck would have it, the Japanese must have been advancing on roads parallel to ours. Occasionally we met a villager; none had seen any Japanese troops. We came to a crossroads where half a dozen Australians, sitting around two machine guns, seemed as lost as we were. They offered us bottles of lukewarm Aussie beer and candy bars. When darkness fell, our expedition ended. We all breathed a sigh of relief and returned to base.

After the war, I learned that the numbers on the enemy's side had been inferior to our own. But our military command was caught completely off guard. Throughout, our generals sought to reassure the population by issuing martial-sounding bulletins that in fact reassured nobody. Even when the Japanese had conquered almost all of Southeast Asia north of us, including some strategically important airfields, ports, and oilfields on the other Dutch islands, our radio was still boasting that we would halt the enemy. One of our military leaders proclaimed, "It is better to die standing up than to live on your knees." When we heard this, we laughed.

As in most peacetime armies, our officer corps had grown smug and fat. In a peaceful society, limiting one's military resources is a good idea. But in the Dutch Indies, the lack of military preparedness stemmed from a deeper cause. When indigenous tribes rebelled, it had always been easy for the colonial army to put them back in their proper place. Local uprisings never got very far. That is how the military had always earned its keep. The resulting complacency had made it doubly difficult for the army to contemplate the possibility that the Japanese might pose a threat. They had managed to convince themselves that Western military power would always be superior to that of Japan, the upstart Asian newcomer, and an inferior race to boot. Most of our officers could not imagine that colonial life would ever come to an end. Thus, the breakneck speed with which the invaders took island after island and conquered country after country left the Europeans in the region shaking in their boots. Their state of utter unpreparedness was not only physical or material; it was psychological as well.

Soon after the outbreak of hostilities in the Pacific region, the Allies established a regional joint American/ Australian/British/Dutch command. It was a hodgepodge of generals, admirals, and air force brass who had never worked together before but soon concluded that Java was indefensible.

On March 8, a week after the invasion began, we heard over the radio that our army had capitulated. It was May 1940 all over again. First the Germans, now the Japanese. Few soldiers on our side had fired a shot. I certainly had not.

A hand-delivered packet from my parents, probably carried in relay from village to village, made it through. It contained, among other things, one of the few notes I had ever received from Father. In my first eighteen years, I had lived in such close proximity to my parents that there was no need to write — except for Mother's daily postcards when she was on a buying trip.

Father reported that, despite what I might have heard about looting in Batavia, they had not been bothered and were both well. I was relieved to hear that. Some of my friends had been distressed to learn that mobs of local Javanese had gone on a rampage, killing, looting, and raping, not only in the Chinese parts of town but also in the Western neighborhood where their parents lived. A letter from Mother and a wad of banknotes was enclosed as well.

In the rest of the week that it took the Japanese to occupy Java, we were confined to barracks. The Japanese had issued orders that all military personnel were to stay put and warned that we would be held accountable for any missing equipment and weapons. They may have got

wind of the desertion of many native soldiers who had simply stepped out of their uniforms, put on civilian garb, and
gone home. In our barracks, much time was spent by the
rest of us lining up for inspection by our sergeant-major
and his superiors, who wanted to make certain that we
were well drilled and disciplined and looking spick and
span. They also made sure that we still had in our possession every article of clothing and every eating implement
that the army had issued us with. I noticed that our officers
now fussed over us more than ever before. It was obvious
that they were as anxious as we were. We were certain, of
course, that the Japanese would intern us. We wondered
how we would be treated.

I had come to another crisis point in my life. I recognized the symptoms from the way I felt when Holland capitulated to the Germans. Once again, my throat and
stomach constricted. I could not express my fear. My
friends and I vented our frustration on everyone in command — our government, the military, and even our own
officers. In the middle of one heated argument, someone
shouted that the radio had just announced that the Americans and Australians would soon counterattack, that, if the
Japanese were to intern us, our captivity would be of short
duration. Most importantly, the war was soon to be over. A
cheer went up. We all believed it. Within a few hours our
euphoria evaporated as the realization sank in that help
was not on the way. We had lost our freedom. We had
no idea what would happen to us now. I had never met a

German soldier and had yet to meet my first Japanese. My thoughts, once again, turned to escape.

On March 9, at 5 A.M., less than twenty-four hours after our surrender, I decided to flee. "If we don't make it, we can always come back," I said to Hans, my high school friend. In our youthful obliviousness, we gave no thought to the possibility we might be killed. We jumped into an open staff car that had the keys in the ignition. Hans drove, since I had never learned how to. The story we made up for the guard at the gate was that the officer who drove this vehicle had ordered us to collect some clothes from his home for laundering. What we did not reveal to him was that our destination was Australia.

Since we had heard on the radio that the Japanese had occupied all ports on the north coast of Java, we headed for Tjilatjap, the southernmost port. There were few vehicles on the road we had chosen.

We did not get very far. Just outside of town on the main road south we were halted at a roadblock manned by Dutch soldiers. An angry young lieutenant, only a year or two older than I, asked to see our orders. We had none. We tried to explain, but to no avail. We were deserters and should be court-martialed, he said. He was still reading us the riot act when a middle-aged captain came up. Luckily for us, he was more sympathetic to our argument. If Dutch soldiers who had escaped the Nazi occupation and reached England could be regarded as heroes, we argued, why then shouldn't *we* be given a chance to escape the Japanese and carry on the fight from somewhere else?

"Let's arrest them," the lieutenant said. But the captain, relenting, allowed us to return to our base. "I have children myself," he said.

As it happened, luck once again saved my life. If Hans and I *had* managed to reach Tjilatjap in time to board one of the last departing vessels, some heading for Australia, others for Sri Lanka, we would have been torpedoed. Japanese submarines sunk every one of those ships. There were no survivors.

4

Prison

A DAY OR TWO AFTER OUR ARMY'S CAPITULATION, a sizable group of older men, most of them in their thirties or forties, had taken occupancy of an empty building in our barracks. They belonged to the volunteer reserves and, like ourselves, had seen no military action. They were teachers, traders, planters, bankers, civil servants, a few clergymen — the backbone of colonial society. Now these men too found themselves in a new and unexpected situation. They had a hard time adjusting to the fact that for the first time in their lives in the Indies, they were no longer in control of their own destiny. Tensions arose between them and the camp command; the civilians held all professional soldiers in contempt and were particularly resentful of the role-reversal foisted on them. In peacetime, the civilians' standard of living far outclassed that of the military. Now it was the officers who enjoyed all the privileges: they were better housed, better fed, and had batmen (orderlies) to wait on them. Adding insult to injury, the officers could boss around the lowly privates — including the new arrivals.

As time went on, I was invited into a regular daily bridge game in the reservists' quarters and listened with a mixture of respect and skepticism to their observations about the native population. In their opinion, the Javanese soldiers had deserted only to become guerilla fighters. They seemed oblivious to the anticolonial resentment that must have been bottled up inside many of the Indonesians. They did not consider the possibility that the natives might have decided this was not their war. It was clear to even a green eighteen-year-old like me that their judgment of the situation had little connection with reality. In the prewar colonial era the white man spoke patronizingly of "his" natives. I could see the two parallel civilizations that coexisted — one representing the master, the other the servant. It was a fragile edifice that could well crumble at any time. I kept my criticisms and irritations to myself, however, for I felt flattered to be invited to participate in their game and enjoyed being treated like a younger brother.

Meanwhile we had been ordered to stay inside our barracks. There was no sign of the Japanese. Several days went by before the Japanese made their presence felt in Bandung. At first a Japanese patrol would enter our compound every day at noon, stay for half an hour, and then leave. Occasionally we received visits from other soldiers. Victors and vanquished were sizing each other up. To us, all Japanese seemed like tourists from a faraway continent: we felt like a spectacle — the human conquests. Some of these tourists were dressed in khaki and all buttoned up; others — wheeling their bikes by hand, rifle slung across the shoulder — wore little more than rags. These were the combat troops who looked as if they had just emerged from the rain forest. The Japanese use of infantry-on-bicycle had proved an innovative military tactic.

In their rapid thrust southward, small bike-mobile Japanese units had moved swiftly along the dirt roads and footpaths of Malaysia, using shortcuts through the jungle that enabled them to avoid defending British troops. They were dressed in little more than loincloths. Others, more conventionally dressed, seemed uncomfortable in the tropical heat, and we learned these had come straight from the cold northern battlefields of China or the winter of their homeland. But every Japanese soldier we saw had a bayonet fixed to his rifle. To us, they were an unappealing and menacing mob; in short, ugly.

Slowly, the Japanese began confiscating our weapons. First they took away our artillery, the antitank guns and the howitzers. Then they ordered us to round up all our rifles, machine guns, revolvers, and knives. We loaded our weapons onto our own trucks, stacking them efficiently in neat piles. Our trucks now bore the emblem of the rising sun. The work was supervised by our own officers, some of whom struck me as acting rather more subservient to the Japanese than was necessary. As the Japanese began barking out their orders more loudly, thereby letting us know that we were not moving fast enough, our own officers began to yell at us too. Our officers' display of fear seemed undignified to me. It betrayed their tendency to brown-nose.

Frans, one of my close friends, was the first of us to receive a beating. Whether by accident or in a spirit of sabotage, he dropped half a dozen rifles that had been tied in a bundle. A Japanese soldier administered some energetic wallops to Frans's face and body, seeming to become more and more agitated. Meanwhile, his mates were hustling the rest of us — pushing and shoving us, gesturing that we should get on with the job and pay no attention to what was happening to Frans. We were seething, but we were also scared; to a man we complied. The next day it was my turn. I have forgotten what it was that I did that resulted in the first beating of my life, but I have never forgotten my outrage. Afterward, I walked around in a daze, hurt and full of anger, especially at my own officers. Not one of them acknowledged what had occurred — there was not a word of protest, nor a gesture of compassion. Months later I could still feel the sting of a fist on my face. For the first time in my life, I felt capable of killing someone. My vengeful fantasies about the Germans at the outbreak of the war had been mild in comparison to my vindictive flights of fancy now, in which the guard who had beaten me received a whipping he would never forget.

Neither the Japanese guards nor any of us prisoners made an effort to communicate. From the very start we were two separate groups. Neither side took even the smallest grain of human interest in the other.

Fortunately, most of the time our captors left us alone. We kept ourselves busy with sports and games. There were soccer matches, at which I was a spectator, and bridge tournaments, in which I was a competitor. In the evening hours we strained our ears trying to interpret the faint and crackling sounds coming from our clandestine radio, which was tuned to a distant Australian frequency. Although there wasn't much in the news to cheer us up, we saw our defeat as a very short-term proposition. The war would end soon, and we would pick up the threads of our normal lives.

Every day a throng of prisoners gathered at the large open window of a building that jutted out into the street in front of our barracks. Here prisoners and their families could communicate, although at a distance. Two lines would form; one inside, the other outside our camp. Cries of greeting, declarations of love, and mimed reports of the state of one's health were exchanged. When a soldier had finished communicating his brief message to his wife, parent, or other loved one, both parties would cede their places at the front of the queue to the persons next in line. The system worked efficiently, without any preset rules.

Although I had assumed that there was no longer any way to get to Bandung from Batavia, Mother showed up one day. There she was, a small figure in a plain white cotton dress (she did not want to appear conspicuous), wiping her face, waving and beaming, and carrying a large basket.

"Are you okay?" she mouthed.

"I'm fine," I responded. "How is Father?"

"Fine, he's fine" she said succinctly. "He is not interned, and I'm fine too. Don't worry. We're both okay." She went on to repeat her question about my health at least half a dozen times.

The basket contained some khaki shirts, underwear, socks, cartons of cigarettes, and canned goods. It was the last gift I would receive in three years. It would be almost four years before I saw Mother again.

(The image of Mother outside the gate of our barracks has stayed with me forever. Often as a boy and later as an adolescent and grown man I was embarrassed and bothered by her love. I experienced her critically as the one person who, oblivious of any friend, neighbor, or colleague who might overhear her, would blurt out whatever came into her mind — usually a recollection of something cute I had said or done when I was little. She always seemed to me a huge, overpowering creature, threatening to smother me in her heavy embrace. It was years before I could see her in a different light, as a courageous and loving, small but determined lady who stood for hours perspiring in the tropical midday sun, waiting patiently to catch a glimpse of me and throw me a kiss. I was ashamed that I had failed to recognize her utter devotion.)

Our peace and quiet lasted for about two weeks. Then, early one morning at daybreak, a large new contingent of guards arrived. The combat troops had gone on to fight other battles; these new soldiers were the occupying force — our jailers. They immediately began patrolling the perimeter of our camp, installed a barbed-wire checkpoint at the gate, set up sentry posts at the corners, and summoned us to an eight o'clock roll call. Whereas the previous guards had left us alone most of the time, these new ones were a constantly menacing presence. They shouted at us at the top of their voices; they ran around on the double, rifle in hand, their body language expressing anger, impatience, and contempt.

Just before the eight o'clock muster, a smartly dressed band of Japanese soldiers marched in, escorting a sleek, shiny staff car that had once belonged to the Dutch headquarters staff, none of whom had ever visited us. The vehicle sported a large flag with an equally large red sun on it. Officers in pressed khaki uniforms, open-necked shirts, and polished high boots, one white-gloved hand resting on the hilt of their samurai swords, thronged around the most senior officer — our new commandant and warden — who mounted a small platform. We all stood at attention. You could have heard a pin drop. Then the officer started to bellow at us in Japanese. One of our interpreters translated that all radio receivers were to be turned in immediately. At roll call, we were to bow to the north to pay our respects to the emperor. We were to salute every Japanese soldier we passed. We would be put to work to earn our keep. We were not to have any contact with the outside world, and no one was allowed to enter or leave the camp without the express permission of the commandant. Any infraction on any of these rules would be severely punished; the penalty for attempting to escape was death.

Then he decided to give a little demonstration. Three prisoners had tried to escape from another camp, he said. He grabbed the rifle of one of his soldiers, let out a blood-curdling yell, and ran toward one of his lackeys as if he was going to drive the bayonet into his heart. He stopped just short of his target, and said no more. There was no need for a translation; his pantomime had been clear enough. We all held our breath. I looked around stealthily. My fellow prisoners and I stood erect, our bodies tense. I was scared and had difficulty controlling the trembling of my knees and the nausea that welled up in my stomach. Grimly the commandant walked back to the platform. He stopped again, impassively tossing the rifle at the soldier whose life he had threatened. It was the first time in my life that I was seriously afraid.

After spelling out the Japanese rules of our confinement and the penalty for breaking them, our new Japanese commandant ordered us to continue standing stock still while he outlined his vision of a new world order. The war was almost over, he said. When the time came, we would be sent home to the Netherlands. A victorious Japan would not tolerate either the Dutch, British, Americans, or French in the "Greater East Asia Co-Prosperity Sphere." From the instant the first Japanese soldier had set foot on Java, he said, the Dutch East Indies had ceased to exist. The former Dutch colony was now incorporated into the Japanese Empire. Our fear was quickly replaced by scorn: the man was a raving lunatic.

From the start of the new regime, we had received no new supplies. We placed ourselves on reduced rations. The Japanese seemed to have no immediate intention of replenishing our reserves of rice, sugar, salt, oil, and other provisions. Our doctors took similar precautions: they restricted the dispensing of bandages, aspirin, quinine, and other medicines.

Rumors continued to have a life of their own. For twenty-four hours we lived in a state of euphoria, convinced of the truth of a report that the Americans had landed somewhere on Java. We came down to earth with a bang. No Americans arrived, but three Eurasian privates who attempted to escape that day were caught almost immediately. Our commandant proved true to his word. The next morning they were bayoneted to death. We were driven out of our barracks to witness the event. The Japanese guards were ordered to attend as well. Some of them were smiling and snickering; they seemed to be genuinely enjoying the spectacle. It marked my first encounter with killing and death.

We were all deeply depressed after that. We could not cheer each other up — this was not going to be a picnic. But our dark mood lasted only a few days. My friends and I were young, healthy, and resilient. We were put to work maintaining the camp in spick-and-span order. After work, the soccer league took to the field. A group of amateur actors organized a cabaret, which put on a new show every Saturday night. The teachers and academics began offering courses on a variety of subjects. It was all a concerted effort to keep up morale.

The first labor project the Japanese had in store for us was erecting a double fence around our barracks. The outer one was made of bamboo, the inner one of barbed wire. We were now properly imprisoned and could not see out. I strung barbed wire, and also had the thankless detail of cleaning the latrines used by the Japanese. This was one of the most risky tasks in camp — the Japanese soldiers in charge of our cleaning unit got a little overexcited seeing us on all fours, and beat us with passionate zeal.

We did not understand the behavior of the Japanese at first. Japanese officers, NCOs and privates alike, showed us only one face: cruel, ruthless, and devoid of any humanity. They would beat us up on the slightest pretext, using fist, stick, rifle butt, or boot. They doled out punishments if we failed to salute, if they saw two of us chatting, if they heard us laugh, or most frequently, for no reason that we could discern. Once, at early-morning roll call, several Dutch soldiers were judged to have failed to bow deeply enough in the direction of the Imperial Palace in Tokyo. They were found guilty of disrespect and sentenced to stand at attention under the burning sun until sundown.

What made these Japanese soldiers lash out at us with such excessive fury? By listening carefully to our interpreter, we finally began to understand a few things. In the eyes of the Japanese, we were cowards. We had surrendered too quickly, without a fight. By surviving, we had offended the Japanese sense of honor and propriety. A Japanese warrior who was defeated was expected to take his own life. Suicide meant atonement for the dishonor of defeat, a dishonor that otherwise placed an unbearable burden on a warrior's family and the nation as a whole. We were reminded over and over again that we were alive thanks only to the beneficence of the emperor, and that we were fortunate to be allowed to serve him as his loyal vassals.

Naturally, to us this talk was just so much gibberish. But our captors were so serious about it that we were finally persuaded that they truly believed what they were saying.

In fact, as I later learned, the guidelines for the treatment of POWs came from the very top. Prime Minister Tojo, in a meeting with his defense chiefs in Tokyo in April 1942, personally advocated a policy of humiliating

POWs. He rejected his foreign minister's recommendation, as well as the advice of one of his own senior generals, that Japan should adhere to the standards of the Geneva Convention (a document never signed by the Japanese). Tojo based his decision on the belief that treating POWs harshly would improve the morale of the natives of Southeast Asia and cure them of any respect they might have harbored for their former colonial masters. Europeans and Americans would be put on display, shown to be miserable creatures who, once stripped of their power, were both cowardly and shamefully subservient. On Java this Japanese strategy worked immediately. Many Indonesians were delighted to see the white master, now clothed in tatters, marched through the city streets on his way to some degrading manual labor. There was even applause for the beatings the Japanese guards dished out — the former colonial rulers were finally taken down a peg or two!

Some POWs managed to escape the blows and kicks; others, less fortunate, nursed their injuries for weeks. We suffered collectively; we were also acutely aware of the Japanese contempt for us. At mealtimes, when we were allowed to sit together, and at night, in the darkness of our hut, we returned the compliment.

Before falling asleep, under my torn army-issue mosquito net, I lay thinking of my happy youth, gone forever. I tried to visualize the family celebrations, my summer holidays in the mountains of the Bernese Oberland, on the coast of Dorset, and in the Rhone Valley, near Lyon. I had a vivid picture of my seventeenth birthday party at home in Scheveningen with my friends Jaap and Hans, my cousin Dick and Jules van Hessen, and some of the prettiest girls in my class. I also saw my parents before me: I heard my mother's happy, sometimes forced and exaggerated laugh, and winked back at my father's wry smile. I was growing increasingly concerned about their fate. For the first time in my life, I spent time thinking about my relationship with my parents. I wondered why I had never been closer to Father. We had never talked freely or shared our feelings, except when we discussed world events — all the major political and military developments, subjects of passionate interest to us both. Why had I not told him more about myself? About my friends, about school, my arguments with Mr. Brouwer, the Nazi biology teacher? And why had I never asked this proud and independent man how it felt to be looked on as a refugee, first in London and then in the Indies?

Did I seem as distant to him as he seemed to me? Or was it Mother who had interposed herself between us, preventing us from establishing a closer bond? I tended to think of Mother as always pushing herself to the forefront, as speaking for all of us, always answering her own questions before I could open my mouth. And of her often embarrassing me in front of others. I did worry about her, of course. But I spent even more time dreaming of the beautiful hairdresser's daughter and about walking hand in hand with Marie-France in the woods around Lyon.

It was a time of daydreaming. I fantasized about the nature of my freedom. Would I go back to Holland? Perhaps England was a better place to go to university. Even in wartime, London had seemed a livelier city than The Hague. It never occurred to me to make a life on Java: Asia, I felt, belonged to the Asians. (Of course, I couldn't foresee that throughout the rest of my life I would retain a feeling of nostalgia for the lush Indonesian landscape and the sight and smell of the buildings in the back of our house in Jakarta where our *djongos* and his family had lived.)

At least once a week we were subjected to a harangue delivered by our Japanese camp commander. We would be ordered to stand at attention while a flood of angry Japanese words washed over us. The officer did not pause long enough to allow our Dutch army interpreter to keep up a running translation. We didn't understand a word until, at the very end of the speech, lasting twenty to forty-five minutes, we were given the gist of what had been said — a mixture of profanities, threats of our impending death, and always, an obsequious hymn of praise to the emperor of Japan. While these insults and obscenities were being hurled at us, we had to remain standing rigidly still. The slightest movement put us at risk of a beating by the Japanese privates who walked up and down our ranks, rifle butts at the ready.

The bombastic martial language did not sound too dissimilar from that of Hitler and Joseph Goebbels, whose ranting I had listened to on the radio at home in Scheveningen. The difference was that now I could hear it live, right here in the middle of our campground. Although I tried to shrug off the threats, it often felt as if a noose was being tightened around my neck. I experienced real fear. Compared to this, the crossing from Scheveningen to Dover had been a breeze — a boy's adventure.

Our commandant never tried to persuade us of his point of view, never justified his own actions or those of his superiors and subordinates, nor did he provide an incentive for good behavior. There was no point hoping for better food or medicine, or even the least reward for our obedience. Repeatedly we were told how he and his men were going to punish us for having started the war, for daring to think that we could put up any sort of resistance against the emperor. He and his men were going to see to it that we would all go to hell.

One day, two American merchant marines were pushed out of a truck onto our doorstep, victims of a bureaucratic foul-up that had separated them from several hundred other Americans who had been captured on Java. They were ordered to bunk in my hut. We became fast friends. I taught them the ropes — how to avoid Japanese patrols, which latrine to use at night when a strict curfew was in effect, where cigarettes — of which they carried a large supply — fetched the best price, and where to buy the black-market rarities we all craved: canned corned beef and sardines and sweetened condensed milk. They talked about "back home" and lent me their old copies of the *Saturday Evening Post* and *House & Garden*. Reading these magazines further whetted my appetite for America. My image of that faraway country had been formed by *The Adventures of Huckleberry Finn*, a few Hollywood movies, the music of Benny Goodman and the Andrews Sisters (on whose recordings I used to spend my entire monthly allowance), and a single Duke Ellington concert I'd attended in The Hague, where I had enthusiastically clapped and stamped my feet. Perhaps my admiration for America was an outgrowth of my admiration for all things English. In any case, I took an instant liking to these two Americans, the first I ever got to know. Everywhere in the camps, Americans were called "Yanks," an Australian army designation. I appropriated these two — they became my Yanks.

It took a day to devour, and a week or two to commit to memory, the magazines' pages of mouthwatering food advertisements. I was fascinated by the small-town rural America depicted by Norman Rockwell. (Sometimes I wonder whether I chose to retire near Stockbridge, Massachusetts, where Rockwell lived and worked, because of the indelible visual impression left on me by those *Saturday Evening Post* covers with their enticing depiction of a carefree normality that was so hopelessly unattainable in prison camp.)

After eight months in our old barracks in Bandung, we were given a day's notice to pack up. It was not until well after midnight of the next day that we were marched to the Bandung station. There we boarded a train for an eight-hour journey to a camp just north of Tandjong Priok, Batavia's port and main shipping terminal, where my parents and I had disembarked only about two years earlier.

After three weeks in a camp not dissimilar to our own, we were on the road again, this time on foot. In order to avoid the heat and humidity of the day, we were marched to the docks in the middle of the night, carrying our gear. The roads were completely deserted except for the Japanese staff cars that sped up and down our column. In the night's quiet and darkness, we were not rushed and could proceed at a leisurely pace. When we reached the port, we were herded onto an old and battered Japanese freighter. Close to two thousand men were sardined into several holds next to or on top of each other. My mates and I could only see what was immediately around us: a sea of men in a space so cramped that it was almost impossible to lie down.

The four-day voyage felt like an eternity. Nauseated by the stench of vomit, urine, and feces, soaked in sweat, we nearly suffocated from lack of air. Occasionally the hatch was opened, letting in a blast of heavy and humid tropical air. Then the hatch was closed again. Twice a day, a barrel of watery soup with a few grains of rice floating in it was lowered and distributed in meager portions. Twice a day we climbed a narrow ladder and stood on deck, pressed uncomfortably together, herded by a handful of guards. We were allowed on deck only long enough for a detail of POWs to hose down the hold. On deck there were four smelly stalls. We pleaded to have more time for their use. The response was *kurro!* — Japanese for "hurry up." In less than an hour we were driven back down into our hell down below. The voyage sapped all our strength. Diarrhea was rampant; about half a dozen men died.

As soon as I felt firm land underfoot, my zest for life returned. We had landed in Singapore. On the quayside some of our own men were assigned to hose down the others. Gratefully I undressed and stood naked under a strong jet of water. For the first time in days, I smelled clean and felt invigorated: the filth, sweat, and despair was washed away. But the Japanese were in a hurry again. My shower lasted only a minute. Some of my friends risked a beating by holding their clothes and other belongings under the stream too. Our spirits soared. Refreshed, we were sure that whatever awaited us, nothing could ever be as bad as that crossing.

Trucks ferried us past a large square building surrounded by an imposing wall that one Dutchman who had lived in Singapore identified as the infamous Changi Gaol. When we drove on and it was clear that the prison building was not our destination, he cheered. I let out a yell of relief too, for the building reminded me of the prison around the corner from our home in Scheveningen. Our celebration was short-lived; a few minutes later our convoy came to a halt, and we were ordered to get out of the trucks. We had stopped in the middle of a sprawling complex of two-story stone barracks in a garden-type setting. We were still in Changi, but in an outlying complex where the guards and other prison staff used to be housed.

Thousands of captives — British, Australian, and Dutch — were crowded into our camp. They did not exactly welcome the arrival of another contingent of POWs. A new lot of prisoners came through the same gate at least once a week, further restricting the already overcrowded living and sleeping space.

The barracks were a cosmopolitan mini-metropolis. Bandung had been a provincial backwater compared to Singapore. The POWs who were already there had developed an amazing menu of activities to keep us occupied — from international soccer matches, chess and bridge tournaments, art shows, comedy theater, and classical and jazz concerts to lectures and courses in mathematics, drawing, philosophy, English literature, history of art, ancient and modern history, French, Chinese, and many other subjects.

Not everyone was engaged in intellectual pursuits. Heavy betting was the order of the day among select groups of poker players. Money gained and lost was tallied on scraps of paper; one copy for the winner, one for the loser, to be cashed in when the war was over — in the not too distant future. Hundreds of British pounds in the form of IOUs changed hands. Meanwhile, a much larger crowd found entertainment and stimulation in bingo nights held twice a week.

I played an occasional game of chess and also participated in a bridge tournament. Frans was my partner. We made the quarterfinals before being thoroughly beaten by two British sergeants.

I enrolled in a heavily subscribed course given by a Dutch captain who believed in the symbolic significance of the Egyptian pyramids. He was convinced that the geometry of the pyramids predicted the future. He would cover a blackboard with cubes and triangles and all sorts of diagrams that "proved" that Japan would be defeated within the next sixty to ninety days. I lapped it up. I was drawn both by the prognosis and by the man's charisma. An amiable giant, he presented his case eloquently in a hesitant, high-pitched voice. I had gone to his class originally out of curiosity, for in his younger days he was something of a celebrity, having been an Olympic rowing champion. I had seen his picture in newspapers and magazines: a very tall, thin figure, photographed next to his skiff. He brought so much conviction and enthusiasm to his thesis that he drew more and more listeners as his lecture series went on. Even though I liked to think of myself as a skeptic, I was desperately hoping for one small but convincing clue that my captivity was about to come to an end. My hopes were as irrational as everyone else's. Anybody on any pulpit or soapbox who promised us our liberty was assured of receiving our grateful and undivided attention.

Deep down I was well aware that we were not only clutching at straws — we were seriously deluding ourselves. For we happened to be in possession of some real facts. A hidden radio in our camp kept us informed about the Allies' moves. As 1942 drew to a close, the Allies were still on the defensive. We realized that a counteroffensive that could turn the tide was unlikely to happen before the middle of 1943, or even later. This meant that it might be a year or two before the war was over. But where did that leave us? We did not like to think in terms of a two-year time frame. Anything beyond a month was the distant future. That was why the lecture series on the pyramids continued to draw record crowds.

In Singapore the Japanese guards were much less in evidence than they had been on Java. For one, the prison encampment itself was much larger, and there were many more POWs milling around the open spaces between the barracks, kitchens, hospital, and storage sheds. The British command apparently had worked out a modus vivendi with the Japanese commander that left the Westerners more or less in control of our daily lives. But our autonomy had not come about without a heavy price.

Before our group arrived, there had been a rebellion in one of Singapore's POW work camps. The POWs had each been ordered to sign a declaration that read: "I

solemnly swear on my honor that I will not, under any circumstances, attempt to escape." The order was met with a
stubborn and general refusal. The standoff lasted six days.
The Japanese made the 15,000 prisoners stand at attention
for long stretches of time, squeezed into one small courtyard. They reduced the sparse food rations, allowed only
the stingiest supply of water, and made the men dig a
wide, deep ditch, ostensibly for a latrine. The implied
threat was that in case of further "lack of cooperation," the
ditches would serve as the POWs' final resting place. To a
nervous and demoralized mob, it spelled mass execution.
The Japanese turned up the pressure several notches by
executing four men who had attempted to escape. All the
prisoners had been herded into the congested parade
grounds to witness the executions. It was made clear to the
British commander that no man would be allowed to leave
until every prisoner had signed. He finally decided that there
was nothing for it but to comply. Besides, they were sign-
ing under duress, so the document's legitimacy was moot.

A British officer friend told me that it was an officer's
duty to escape. Although not an officer myself, I considered
myself an experienced escape artist. I became obsessed
with the notion of flight. But as I was enclosed within a vast
Asian continent, surrounded by people of different color
and size, and separated from friendly forces by at least a
thousand miles, all dreams of escape remained a fantasy.

All of us, including the British officers, finally faced

the reality: escape was impossible. The British officer corps had been dealt another psychological blow: some of their formerly loyal Sikhs and other Indian regiments had switched their allegiance to the Japanese. As in the case of our native Indonesian soldiers, the Sikhs' secret, long-suppressed grudges against their white officers, coupled with self-interest, won out over loyalty. Not that any real hope of freedom was ever held out to them; their defection was rewarded only by a policy of reverse racial discrimination. Their new Japanese masters gloated when the bearded and turbaned Sikh soldiers, until a few months earlier the pride of the British Empire, jumped at the chance of tying up a young British officer and giving him a sound beating.

Whenever a POW ran into a Japanese soldier, it was a tense moment. The Japanese insisted on the proper salute — an obsequious reverence that was required of us as the defeated. If you failed to deliver, you risked a blow, a kick, or both. If a POW then failed to put on a suitable show of contrition, a full-scale beating would follow. A young Australian sergeant, after a severe beating by two Japanese soldiers, was thrown into solitary confinement with little water and no food. He was never told anything further about the nature of his offense, and his officers met no success in seeking an explanation. After three days the young Australian was discharged from his private prison and taken to our hospital, where he died. The Japanese treatment of POWs ruled out any recourse under any kind of military law. Protests were useless.

The true heroes in our camp were the radio operators — the men who, once a week in the dead of night, put on their headsets, memorized what they heard, and passed on that information to two or three trusted friends. These, in turn, disseminated the snippets of news, giving us the illusion that we were still in touch with the outside world. The optimistic news picked up from the British station in New Delhi sounded completely reliable to us. It did not occur to anyone that our side might also be engaging in a little wartime propaganda.

After the broadcast, the set would be totally disassembled; some parts were buried in the ground, others hidden in water bottles, sick-bay supplies, and kitchenware. Some of the sets had been constructed from scratch using scavenged parts; others had been imported by the new arrivals from Java and other islands. Later, when the prisoners were dispersed to Burma, Thailand, and Japan, the sets would travel again, accompanying their owner-operators. For the purpose of transportation, some sensitive parts of the human body were put to good use; orifices such as armpit and anus proved useful, as did the Australian wide-brimmed hat and the jockstrap.

I had an Australian mate who kept me informed. One day he seemed chagrined, and although he had always been very circumspect about divulging details of the clandestine radio operation, he now confided in me that the attempt to receive news from an Australian station had failed once again. The New Delhi frequency that relied on the BBC for its news remained our sole, treasured, and relatively clear source of information for all that was happening around the world.

After our morning ablutions, we would try to capture adjoining latrines so that he could whisper to me what had been heard the night before. I never learned who my friend's source was. I was just one small link that transmitted the news headlines to a larger chain, whose members had been appointed by someone higher up in our hierarchy and whose identity was to be kept secret. My Australian informant instructed me to pass on the news verbally to a Dutch lieutenant. I had the feeling that, in our system of internal transmission, the positive news was embellished bit by bit, while the negative was somewhat discounted.

The Japanese suspected the existence of a radio and carried out frequent unannounced inspections. They made it clear that they knew what we were up to. But neither the set itself nor any of its parts were ever found.

My original contact with the Australian had been through the black market. I became a middleman, operating on the fringes. Upon my arrival in Changi I heard from other POWs that the different camp commanders had followed varying policies regarding their prisoners' property. Some allowed their men to rob the POWs blind, leaving the prisoners only the clothes on their back; others had issued strict orders forbidding their subordinates to take any valuables, such as money, watches, and rings, from the prisoners. In the camps I had been in on Java, we had been lucky. We had been allowed to keep our valuables. I proudly wore my Omega watch, with a lizard strap, a seventeenth-birthday present from my parents.

Trading, in the form of barter, had started at the very beginning of our captivity. On Java, the biggest demand had been for cigarettes, followed by candy and Western-type canned foods. Before we were moved from our original barracks, most of us had possessed several pairs of shoes and belts and civilian neckties and shirts. And we all had money. With each move, we shed some of our clothing, trying to sell the best pieces. By the time I arrived in Singapore, I owned only what I wore, plus a spare shirt and a spare set of underwear and socks — and my puttees, an itchy, uncomfortably hot article of ornamental military clothing worn around the legs. I had never learned how to put them on properly; they always sagged below my knees so that I constantly had to pull them up again. Even though I had given up wearing them, they had become part of me; they were my security blanket, and I held on to them for dear life.

When all our cash was gone, we were left with our watches. The Japanese showed an insatiable hunger for famous name brands: Rolex, Omega, Patek Philippe, and Longines. When our supply of the more expensive fourteen- and eighteen-carat pieces had run out, they offered good prices for simpler watches in silver or steel. They paid cash for the expensive items; more modest purchases were paid for with a basket of leftover change, cigarettes, or canned foods. On those nights when a trustworthy Japanese guard was on duty (i.e., one who was in on the racket), he would look the other way as two POW trade emissaries risked their lives by slipping through a gate and striking deals with the Chinese tradesmen lurking just outside the prison grounds. Before slinking back, they would set a date for the next session. They brought back burlap bags full of cigarettes, condensed milk, corned beef, sardines, jam, and other commodities. I have always been amazed that, as far as I know, no one was ever caught; neither the POWs nor the Chinese black marketeers.

I traded in my own beautiful eighteen-karat Omega, that treasured birthday present from my parents, for a hefty sum and managed to spend it all very quickly. At first I felt depressed and full of self-reproach at having parted with my most precious possession. But once I had accumulated a small stock of cigarettes and luxury goods. I was convinced that with these easily salable items, I had gained some economic security. My dozen cans of corned beef and sardines would bring a good price when traded for bananas and other perishables.

Haggling over the price of my Omega had given me a sense of satisfaction that my stints at Hatton Garden and Borsumij had failed to evoke. I decided to join the black market as a middleman and began to trade in watches. In return for obtaining a good price for a POW's most precious asset, I received a 5-to-10-percent commission. I would be entrusted with a watch by a friend or a friend of a friend and take the merchandise to a hut at the other side of the camp where Max, one of the camp's most successful dealers, held court. My consignors trusted me to obtain the best value for them, and I was given carte blanche in my negotiations. Max would make a low first offer for the watch in response to what I considered my own reasonable opening bid. Each transaction lasted an hour or more before we reached an agreement.

Max, lording it over a network of middlemen like myself, seemed to like me. His approval meant a lot to me. He made me feel triumphant each time I made a sale. He looked like the stereotyped caricature of a successful and well-fed businessman: heavyset, with bulging eyes shaded by black eyebrows, always chewing on a big cigar. Before the war he had been a junior trader at Internatio, the largest trading company in the Dutch East Indies. Welcoming me as a fledgling colleague from the rival Borsumij, Max took me under his wing. He impressed on me that my former employer was a lowly number-two Avis compared to his Hertz. There was a price to be paid for being in his company: I had to listen to long-winded monologues on the incestuous relationships among competitors in our colonial economy. Max was at least five years older than I was and claimed to have studied economics. I became one of his hangers-on, with whom he shared his opulent supply of cigarettes, cigars, and foodstuffs. For all his bluster and self-importance, I soon learned that Max himself was merely a junior partner in the whole risky enterprise of watch disposal. He loved to give the impression that he was at the top of a POW hierarchy that inspected and evaluated every watch brought to market: the final price, however, was determined by a Scottish sergeant-major who closed the deals with a Japanese counterpart.

Meanwhile, we had moved again and I was now in the main Changi prison building. Seven days a week, work parties left Changi to unload ships in the harbor or to help with the construction of new runways at the airport. My own Java contingent was mysteriously excused from hard labor. Our boring task was to clean up the courtyard and the prison corridors. During the day we were joined by other POWs who had not been picked for work detail that day, and who milled around aimlessly. At night, the place was packed: a prison built by the British to hold 600 inmates now housed close to 12,000.

For all the crowding here, we lived an almost autonomous existence under a near-benign regime — a marked contrast to our previous camps on Java. I was eager to learn as much as I could. I ran from a seminar on the bright future of the British Empire to an Australian captain's objective analysis of the Japanese strategy in overrunning the Malay peninsula, then on to a private tutorial in conversational French. I was also an active participant in our POW theatrics. On any given evening I could be found rehearsing for one of the cabaret shows we put on. Some members of the cast were semiprofessionals or experienced amateurs who not only acted but wrote and composed sketches and songs. The bulk of the material was nostalgic and very British, since a major proportion of the POWs in Changi belonged to British units that had arrived just before the Japanese onslaught. There was plenty of Noel Coward and an abundance of Vera Lynn. Original texts by amateur writers like myself contained a profusion of sexual innuendo. I felt very proud when a silly skit I wrote about a husband, his wife, and a seductive maid was put on; I got to play the small role of the husband in it. My ten-minute piece received a lukewarm response. The hit of the show was a star turn by a slender, effeminate Dutch Eurasian who starred as a female impersonator. He/she also played the maid in my piece as well as every other female role. He brought the house down every time: the audience would roar its approval at each wiggle.

The programs changed every four to six weeks. The Japanese officers would attend at least one performance of each new show. Seated in the front rows, they would leave immediately after the last number before the intermission: the slot reserved for our sexy star's hula dance. After the Japanese had gone and we had the place to ourselves, a team of Cockney comedians would recite a litany of wickedly broad and scatological jokes about our captors. They would sprinkle their dialogue with a liberal application of four-letter words. Our audience went wild, cheering on the two men on the stage, who were able to express so eloquently our collective feelings of resentment and frustration.

Frans was my closest friend in Changi Gaol. He was a cheerful man bubbling over with joie de vivre. That is what attracted me to him. Together we were a clown act — laughing at our own jokes and making other prisoners laugh too.

Before the war, Frans had flunked out of medical school. In 1939, he had worked as a steward on the Holland America Line. He had made just one round-trip transatlantic crossing from Rotterdam to Hoboken before the war broke out. Then his ship, converted to a troop transport, participated in the British evacuation of Crete. German planes set fire to his ship; Frans jumped overboard and was rescued and set ashore in Alexandria. After an adventurous journey through India, he arrived on Java just in time to be drafted into our army.

Women had apparently found this tall, wiry, blond Dutch kid with his big ears, athletic build, and constant wide smile irresistible. Frans often entertained us with his tales of seduction. He claimed to be unsuccessful in warding off the advances women made to him. He had us in stitches with his tales of playing the reluctant lover. His exploits featured Dutch students and waitresses; a middle-aged widow aboard his ocean liner who, clad only in a pearl necklace, had invited him into her first-class cabin; and a whole string of Egyptians, Indians, and other exotic types. It was a 1940s version of *The Decameron*. Others chimed in with descriptions of their own sexual adventures. We gobbled it all up eagerly.

But Frans's wide grin, which had helped him seduce so many girls and women, also began to attract the attention of the Japanese guards. Frans's radiant personality was his undoing. It was as if he provoked, and he was regularly beaten up. Japanese patrols circulated throughout the camp at irregular intervals, and although all his friends warned him to stay out of their way, Frans preferred to live dangerously. We began to suspect that it was not only his smile but also his size — he was a very big man — that made him a target for their abuse. My friends and I concluded that the Japanese had a special antipathy toward tall Westerners; they disliked them even more than short soldiers like me. For a Japanese guard, a tall man was a challenge — harder to slap in the face, yet offering the pleasurable alternative of punching him below the belt.

In the months that followed, Frans became a routine target. Without bothering to find a pretext, the Japanese would attack him for no reason at all. One night I heard the big man quietly sobbing. Frans was my *slaapie*, a term used in the military for bedfellow, the fellow who bunked next to you. I put my hand on his arm. The sobbing stopped. Frans climbed into my bunk and lay next to me. We fell asleep, back to back, comforted by the warmth of each other's bodies.

"I envy you," Frans once said. I was short, reserved,

self-effacing, and easily lost in the crowd. It helped. I was not singled out for too many beatings.

A strong bond grew between us. We took our meals together; at night I could hear him snore or feel him toss restlessly. Yet we were not tempted to experiment in any sexual way. Our meager diet must have had something to do with it, weakening our sex drive; but a sense of propriety held us back as well. Occasionally I would wake up in the early morning with an erection, as in former days. But that would soon vanish, together with its accompanying sexual fantasy, which usually focused on Marie-France or some girl from the distant past but which could never be transferred to the miserable, abused, and battered creature with whom I sometimes lay back to back.

Frans's size proved to be his undoing. He was taken out of our group and selected to join the first work party that left Changi. His group, we were told, was going on a permanent mission to an unknown destination. He was the first of my friends to die on the railroad.

Driven by adolescent hyperactivity and a need for stimulation, I conceived the idea of starting a restaurant. The goal was to raise money for the purchase of medicines, since our stock was running low. I presented a proposal that was sketchy but basically sound to two British officers, one of whom was in charge of drug supplies, the other of miscellaneous entertainment projects. It was the first business presentation I had ever made in my life. I felt elated when I obtained the go-ahead. A site was selected. We furnished it with long benches and a few small tables under a large bamboo overhang. Half a dozen cooks working under a Dutch Eurasian chef cooked over open fires. Supplies were limited: bananas, rice, coconuts, sugar, salt, oil, and a few eggs. Consequently the menu was limited as well; our most popular item was *ongol ongol*, a jellied and slippery pudding made of coconut milk, coconut rind, and sugar. Our regular camp kitchen hardly ever provided sweets; we all craved sugar. It came as no surprise, therefore, that every evening a long line would form in front of our cafe's cashier, who used an old cigar box as his cash register. We had to impose a limit of two *ongol ongols* per person. The rest of the menu, which might feature a minuscule portion of banana fritters or saucer-sized mini-omelettes with a pinch of salt, was dependent not only on what ingredients were available but also on the whim of the chef, a young man of great talent and a dazzling smile. I named the restaurant the Flying Dutchman.

It became fashionable to have a snack at the new café/ restaurant after our meager six o'clock supper and before the nine o'clock curfew. The venture became much more popular than expected. It was all the rage to have dessert at our place, where one could chat, nibble, and listen to a variety of entertainers, accompanied by a guitar player.

Meanwhile, the black market was thriving — and expanding. With most watches gone, Parker pens, cigarette lighters, cuff links, and silver pencils became popular with the Japanese. Working outside the perimeter of our jail, members of the work parties stole whatever they could get their hands on: screwdrivers and other small tools, light-bulbs and flashlights. They became very skilled at snatching salable merchandise right from under the noses of their Japanese guards and finding ingenious ways to hide these in their clothing or mess tins until the time came to hand over the loot to their equally clever fences: their Singaporean Chinese black-market contacts.

A good thing finally came to an end. In the last months of 1942 and the first four months of 1943, more and more POWs, my original Java contingent among them, were sent out on successive rail transports. Because I was "manager" of the Flying Dutchman, I was considered staff and, at first, exempted from the regular deportation of prisoners destined for "up country." The Japanese told us that we were being sent to work in the north, but supplied no further details. Those of us still in Changi, including hundreds of Allied officers, were organized into a group designated as H-Force.

By May 1943, our restaurant had shut down. There were neither enough cooks nor enough customers left. My unit, including the entire staff of the Flying Dutchman, was on one of the last trains out. Except for the hospital, Changi was now virtually empty.

My bunkmate George stood beside me, as he had at every roll call in Changi, while a Japanese soldier counted us for the last time in the place that had become home to us. George and I had never had much to say to each other. George looked like an old man to me. He must have been in his late twenties and had been deputy manager of a tea plantation in eastern Java. When we were finally told to pack up, he shaved off his mustache. "Too much work," he explained. "Besides, I'm not going to survive." He was in an almost constant state of depression. That was the main reason for our not getting along at first: to me, he was an old grouch; to him, I was the naive and eternal optimist.

By this time, however, we had gradually come to respect each other — George appreciated my energy, I his wide knowledge of botany, which he used to teach to a large class of POW students.

Whereas my attitude toward life was that the glass was half full, George's glass was always half empty. It was a difference in outlook: the view of the "old" George versus that of the young nineteen-year-olds. I had become impatient with the men of experience in our midst (those in their thirties and early forties!), whom I dismissed for their lack of wisdom, loathed for their lack of optimism, and envied for their self-proclaimed maturity.

The train journey north, across the Malay Peninsula into Thailand, lasted four days and four nights. About thirty men were crowded into our freight car, which stank. Our light gear was piled in a corner. I sat in the center. At first I was jealous of the privileged few who had found a spot where they could rest their back against one of the sides of the car. We were so cramped for space that I soon found myself sitting back to back with George. It turned out that we could give each other some support; we now seemed to be better off and slightly less uncomfortable than those around the edge, who were now jammed into the sides and the doors. At infrequent stops we were allowed to relieve ourselves in ditches dug parallel to the track. We were fed twice a day: a bowl of rice and a soup of watery vegetables. Local vendors offered us bananas and pineapples, and our guards allowed us to make purchases. At one stop a generous group of men and women, members of Malaya's Indian minority, brought us a gift of mangoes and rambutan, a delicious tropical fruit. It was a feast — the last we were to enjoy for a long time.

At first we were surprised that so few Japanese guards accompanied our transport. Evidently, the Japanese were confident that we would not contemplate an escape. In this, they turned out to be right, for although we talked about it, we were too weak, discouraged, and fearful to follow through.

As the journey progressed, conditions deteriorated. Many prisoners were suffering from diarrhea. The suffocating stench grew all but unbearable in the late afternoon, when the temperature had risen over the one-hundred-degree mark.

Toward the end of our journey we were bruised and aching all over from the jostling and jolting. The train made many sudden stops, for no apparent reason; then, just as unpredictably, it would lurch forward again. As the days passed, sitting and squatting became increasingly uncomfortable. It felt as if my back was broken. Added to the pain, thirst, and hunger was apprehension about what awaited us. We wanted the ride to be over. The sea voyage from Java to Singapore had taken an unexpected twist: it had ended in the Changi compound, where the living conditions were better than on Java. A similar fate might very well await us now. But we were nervous all the same.

Our final stop was Bangpong, a village in southern Thailand, about forty miles west of Bangkok. Here was the starting point of one of Japan's major strategic undertakings: the construction of a 350-mile railroad through the jungle. It was to be a direct link between the ports of Thailand and the front in Burma. From there the Japanese aimed to conquer India. This was the infamous Thailand-Burma railroad — and we were to be the slave labor that built it, yard by yard, mile by mile, through an impenetrable jungle.

(In 1939 the Japanese had decided that, to ensure a successful invasion of India, their navy would have to exercise control over the waters west of Singapore and the Malay Peninsula. The Japanese navy had to provide guaranteed access to Rangoon, capital of Burma, the nearest major port to India, where huge Japanese armies and their materiel could come, and from which they could launch their offensive against the British in India. If a hitch occurred, it would be necessary to supply the invading army by rail from Bangkok. A railroad starting in Bangkok and leading through the Thai and Burmese jungles became Japan's backup plan. Japanese engineers had estimated that it would require two years to build. After the Japanese lost the battle of Midway, the Japanese high command was compelled to conclude — and did so hesitatingly — that the Japanese fleet had failed to deliver; control of the sea routes leading to Rangoon had been lost. The railway now became the highest priority. The time for construction was cut in half: the engineers were given eighteen months to complete the project. A few months into the job, the deadline for completion was reduced even further, to just one year. It was decided that this could be accomplished through the use of a massive captive labor force composed of POWs and indigenous workers from the "liberated" Asian territories. At the same time, the use of captive Allied manpower solved a logistic problem that the Japanese had not anticipated — they had never expected to be saddled with such a large number of POWs who needed to be fed and guarded, putting a cumbersome burden on Japan's shrinking wartime resources.)

When we got off the train, we entered a dramatically different world — poorer, dirtier, and smellier than anything I had seen in any of the towns and villages of Indonesia. Bangpong, the village through which we marched, did not contain a single proper building — each of its bamboo huts, along which we passed, was ramshackle. Everything looked filthy. We saw low huts with thinly thatched roofs of palm leaf that provided no protection from the tropical downpours. The earth was black and muddy; mangy dogs and cats moved about freely. When we got to the transit camp for the prisoners, we found that it was no improvement over the town. Inside our huts were thousands of mosquitoes hiding in the rafters, waiting for the right moment to bite. Clouds of blackflies and bluebottles hovered over shallow, unhygienic latrines. Our dwindling supply of cash was good for something at least; toward the beginning of our stay we were able to buy eggs and some fruit. Our large transit camp was also named Bangpong. Even though we had suffered hardship in Java and undernourishment in Changi, our physical surroundings there had been familiar: the overcrowded barracks had been of a roomy Western-influenced design and well constructed. This was different — a general sense of gloom descended on us.

My own dismay was mixed with curiosity; perhaps the scene did not fill me with as much gloom as it did many older POWs. But there was no good news — British POWs who told us that they were semipermanent staff expressed a sense of isolation that had not existed in Changi. We realized that we were now really in the middle of nowhere. Matters were only made worse when we were assured that there was no prospect of being sent to a place that would be any better. I consoled myself with the thought that the war would soon be over. This was easily done, considering the absence of news other than the Japanese propaganda reported in a Thai newspaper, which was sporadically smuggled into the compound. Apparently no one had yet dared to reassemble the radio receiver.

Back in Singapore, we had heard rumors about the labor camps — that life there was hard — but there had been no specific details. Within our first half hour in Bangpom, we learned from the "staff" and from prisoners who had arrived a week before us that we would be working on a railroad that was far from finished; that "up country" there was even less food and fewer medicines; that the Japanese would make us work as hard as we could; that we would be beaten; and that many men had died. I had a few anxious moments, but those soon passed. The prospect of death was so unappealing that I chose to ignore it: life, I thought, was bound to go on somehow until my new and real life would start, after the war was over.

In all, the Japanese brought about 200,000 Malays, Tamils, Chinese, Javanese, and other natives of Indonesia to Thailand, together with 61,000 Allied POWs, to form a slave labor force numbering more than a quarter of a million men. Personally, I never met any of the Asians who labored on the railroad. But they were there all right. Their fate — in terms both of fatalities and of suffering — was even worse than that of the POWs. It has been estimated that the death rate among the hundreds of thousands of Asian workers on the Burma Road, many of them accompanied by their wives and children, was as high as 80 to 90 percent.

In Bangpong I met a Dutch acquaintance from
Changi who had arrived two months earlier. Sam was a
prosperous truck driver now. He boasted that he had even
managed to gain weight since his Changi days. He told me
how he traded contraband with yellow-robed Buddhist
priests. Tools and other supplies vital to the construction
of the railroad, he confessed, had a habit of disappearing
from his truck into the jungle. The gang of junior Japanese
officers who organized the operation rewarded the POWs
participating in their racket with extra food supplies.
"When you look beneath the surface," Sam said, "you'll
find that the Japanese are even more corrupt than we are."

His usual cargo was rice. Although the Japanese required a meticulous accounting of the number of bags he
transported, there were ways and means, he said, to skim
off a small quantity from a bag or two. He'd drop this price-
less booty off at one of the POW kitchens. "I'm giving it to
our own and to the Aussies," he said. "Some of them limey
cooks have sticky fingers. They have a habit of keeping
the goodies for themselves." Sam offered to arrange for me
to join him and become a driver as well as a black marke-
teer. It was the only insurance policy, he claimed, against
being sent on to Burma. "There's cholera up there," he said.
"You should avoid those camps at all cost. You go up there,
you're as good as dead." But Sam made me feel nervous,
and I did not quite trust him. "I can't drive," I said. "I can
teach you in an hour," he said. But he could not persuade

me. My longing for new adventures had left me; I preferred to stay with my friends and companions in H-Force.
Also, I had grown accustomed to my friends, a group of men
in whose midst I felt somewhat sheltered and protected.

But the encounter with Sam also left me numb. He
painted a picture of cholera, famine, and brutality. He also
brought me the news that Frans had died of amoebic
dysentery shortly after his arrival in one of the work camps.
He had been a champion to the end, Sam said. The most
beaten-up prisoner of all.

A few days after our arrival in Bangpong we were told
to pack our belongings. At midnight we were ordered to
fall in and start marching. We passed through the gate in
the flimsy fence around the camp of Bangpong, and on
that first leg of our journey we marched for six or seven
hours along a paved road. There were around two or three
hundred prisoners, with half a dozen Japanese in front, an
equal number walking alongside, and another five or six
bringing up the rear. Although weakened, most of us were
able to sustain the brisk pace set by our Japanese guards.
But even on that first night's relatively easy march, some
POWs did not have the stamina to keep up. They were
prodded and beaten by the Japanese rear guard. The Japanese had bayonets fixed to their rifles; some also carried
bamboo clubs, which they used on the stragglers. We
propped up our faltering colleagues as much as our guards
would allow us to and carried their few belongings. The

total distance covered that night was nearly twenty miles. At-one-and-a-half-hour intervals, we were given a ten-minute rest break.

By the second night the paved road had become a rain-soaked muddy trail. For the next couple of nights we walked two or three abreast. Then the road narrowed further, and we had to form a single line that snaked its way through the jungle. Our guards had disbanded into twos and threes and kept up the pace by yelling at us to move faster. Every once in a while a POW would sit down because he could not go on, or would stumble over a branch, or would simply stop, tensed up and near-petrified from exhaustion and the fear of another beating. Whatever the cause that slowed us down, forcing a moment's unauthorized rest, it enraged the Japanese. Cursing obscenities, one of them would push and elbow his way past us to reach the culprit and beat him to a pulp.

On the third day we had our first casualty. After the night's march we were totally exhausted and laid ourselves to rest in the shade of the trees. One of the men had fallen asleep in an open clearing without noticing the rise of the burning sun. He died of sunstroke.

For five interminable nights we proceeded along a single, heavily trodden service road that was nothing but a slippery, overgrown footpath that other groups of POWs had taken before us. We walked parallel to rail beds that were under construction. On the last days our daylight hours were spent in huts intended for transients. These huts were adjacent to more permanent but equally rickety camps that were empty by day because their occupants, our POW colleagues, were out at work. Sometimes we could hear hammering in the distance. After trying to get some sleep in the heat and humidity of the day, we would continue on our laborious march.

It rained hard and steadily most of the time. Streams of water poured down on us from heavy tropical leaves. The ground was strewn with branches and large roots; we stepped across the charred remains of trees felled and burned to make room for the rail bed.

Near the end of our fourth night, we reached a breaking point. It was almost daybreak, and we were just coming to the end of an exhausting, wet, stop-and-go ordeal. The night's march had seemed more difficult and tiring than any we had experienced before. We were ordered to get up again after just five minutes, five minutes short of the (by-now-established) ten-minute rest period we had grown to consider a rightful and nonnegotiable entitlement. Some of the men, completely exhausted, could not get back on their feet. Our Japanese guards flung themselves at them, screaming and kicking. I had already started to move but turned around and ran back to where the shouting and kicking was going on. Together with several others, I started yelling at the Japanese to stop. Either the same idea had come to all of us at the same time, or one man's initiative had prompted a spontaneous reaction in the rest of us. We struck a militant posture. Our guards went on shouting at the top of their lungs. We were shouting, too.

Abruptly the Japanese stopped beating our stragglers. A standoff had been reached; a ragtag band of prisoners facing a solid line of Japanese soldiers, their bayonets aimed at our chests. Their leader barked a command; they lowered their guns and took a step back. "Sit," their sergeant barked in both English and Japanese. We sat. The Japanese crouched, their rifles at the ready. We glared at each other. After two or three minutes of absolute silence, the order was given to move on. We took the weaker prisoners into the middle of our line and soon reached our destination.

The next night was the last of our nightly marches. The Japanese made no further effort to force the pace. Briefly we had won back our self-respect. And for a moment we thought, or liked to believe, that the Japanese saw us through different eyes. We had shown ourselves, we proudly felt, honorable warriors, if only for a fleeting moment. Still, the march cost us a dozen men — companions who died from exhaustion on the trail.

When we finally arrived at the camp that was to be our home for the next six months, we found it empty and far from finished. We gathered in front of two rows of identical, skeletal, and desolate-looking huts. Our own commanding officer asked us to stand in a half-circle around a Dutch Roman Catholic army chaplain who began a prayer.

His words meant nothing to me; in my own way I tried to think of something positive. I looked for any sign of hope I might find in the pinched faces of my fellow POWs, in the trees and bushes surrounding us, or up above, high in the leafy ceiling hovering over the narrow clearing. We were a group of exhausted men huddled together around the chaplain. The sunlight broke through in uneven shafts.

For some never-explained reason, this new prison without walls was the only camp along the railroad that did not have a Thai name. It was called, ironically, Spring Camp.

5

Death Camp

WE HAD WALKED EIGHTY-SIX MILES but were put to work
as soon as we arrived. First, we finished the construction of
our huts, made of bamboo and roofed with *atap* palm leaves.
The interior of the huts was divided into two low platforms
made of split bamboo. We had practically no space on either side. Then we were ordered to clear the jungle from
the muddy overgrown path that was used as a service road
for the railroad under construction. On this badly potholed
road, burlap bags of rice for the prisoners, food and other
supplies for the Japanese guards, and rails and railroad ties
could be delivered by truck.

The hardest and most dangerous part of the job, which
kept us busy for several weeks, was cutting down trees.
The Japanese in charge kept giving contradictory orders.
At one time we were ordered to pull the ropes on a tree
that was to fall in a certain direction; then our guards yelled

at us to run back through thick underbrush to the other side, and pull hard in the opposite direction. No one actually got crushed, but there were several close calls. We grumbled incessantly; our sour mood was not improved by a Japanese command that we were to complete work on our own officers' tent in the middle of the camp first before tackling what our British mates called "digs." In general, though, the crews assigned to construct the rickety structures that would put a leaky roof over our heads displayed significantly more diligence than the road-building teams.

After the trees had been chopped down, I remained part of the crew that maintained our section of the road. It was a never-ending battle, as the heavy daily rains and the rapidly growing tropical vegetation made the road barely passable, even on the best of days. We were responsible for approximately three miles of road. There were flanking POW labor camps on either side (generally, the camps along our section of the Burma Road were from one to six miles apart). We were on the southeastern side of the Thai-Burma border, where at least thirty POW camps were located. In that broad area, the construction activity imposed on the Western military captives was intense. The Japanese plan called for us to be moved later to tackle other parts of the line farther to the northeast. My work with Spring Camp's road crew lasted about two months.

After the access road had reached a passable stage, I was assigned to a unit that chiseled and hammered away at rocks that obstructed the railroad bed. We slaved nine hours a day, with just three short breaks. We were allowed less than an hour of free time, in the late afternoon, after work, and before supper. During the first few weeks, the Japanese, at unpredictable and unexpected intervals, might decide to give half the workers some time off on a Sunday morning or afternoon. In making the brusque announcement that some of us were furloughed for a few precious hours, the guards made it sound as if we had stolen something valuable from the emperor. In those rare free hours, we would engage in an ineffective battle to improve our living conditions — by digging new latrines, for instance, or building a narrow bamboo table down the center of our cramped sleeping quarters. We also tried to secure our hut against the drenching rain, but we did not have enough palm leaf for a proper roof. It is not unusual in this part of the tropics to be pummeled by up to ninety inches of rain during the four-month monsoon season. Insects throve in the oppressive humidity. Our hut was infested with all sorts of flying and crawling creatures. I would be awakened several times during the night by bedbugs. Their bites kept me awake much of the night, despite my physical exhaustion. I would doze off again after crushing a few bugs between my nails. The creatures left a sickly sweet smell.

Our food consisted of three small bowls of rice a day, a thimbleful of overcooked stringy vegetables, an occasional sweet potato, and sporadically, a soup of onions with, even more rarely, a few slivers of meat. The rice that had rotted away (on the open trucks that carried supplies to the camps) further reduced our rations. I soon came down with dysentery. A watery fluid poured out of me every two to three hours, gradually increasing to about fifteen times a day. Others drained themselves forty or fifty times a day. Many died. Throughout the camps the incidence of dysentery assumed epidemic proportions. Because I could stand upright at roll call, I was automatically declared fit for work. But even if I had not been able to stand, I would not have been excused from labor. With few exceptions, the Japanese guards would force the sick to go to work too.

One day, I collapsed and was unable to get up. But it was not dysentery that knocked me off my feet. It was a sudden outbreak of malaria. I was shivering violently and, two days later, began suffering from hallucinations. It was the first time in my life that I had been seriously ill. When the time came to fill the day's quota of POW workers, I could do nothing but lie flat on my back and watch.

A Japanese soldier, accompanied by our Dutch medical officer, walked through our hut to inspect the sick that had been ordered by our doctor to stay in bed. To the Japanese we were all malingerers. The Japanese soldier on duty looked at me for a moment. Blinking, I waited anxiously for the grinning apparition standing by my cubicle to move on. Was he a ghost? The small figure suddenly blew up into a gigantic form, and then shrank back again into a little man, someone my own age, with dark patches of sweat staining his khaki shirt.

Then he barked something and walked on. He drove about a dozen other men from their beds, over the strong protests of our physician. In the course of the morning inspection, our guards took pride in arbitrarily sending some of the most obviously sick and skeleton-like POWs out to work. On some days, twenty to thirty of the two hundred POWs who were too sick to work were pushed and jostled to their workplace.

After the war I learned that the Japanese high command in charge of railway construction had set a policy whereby no more than 15 percent of the available POW manpower was permitted to be sick or absent from labor for any other reason. In Spring Camp the actual number of disabled through sickness must have been 30 to 40 percent of our total strength on any given day. Further, the Japanese command decreed that no prisoner was allowed to have more than one day in bed. The fact that we could not deliver on either requirement infuriated our guards and made them kick us out in the manner of slave drivers throughout history.

During the long workday, the Japanese drove us hard. At dusk, when we got back into our hut, we were mostly silent, too exhausted to talk. Conversation was no longer a solace. When we needed to communicate, we did so tersely and sparingly, speaking softly. In the night all human sound fell silent, and the steady and heavy rainfall drowned the sounds of the jungle out.

I was allowed to rest and recover temporarily. I was

lucky; George, who bunked next to me, was not. His affliction, caused by malnutrition, was beriberi; his belly was bloated, and he had abscesses on both legs and both feet. Day after day, the Japanese guard drove George out of our hut to work. George had an explanation for it: "I am so ugly," he said, "that I offend their concept of aesthetics."

Even in his deepest misery, George's mind raced in all directions. He was nostalgic for his life in Wageningen, a sleepy provincial town in the eastern part of Holland where he had obtained his degree in botany and where, with his beer-drinking fellow students, he had been known to disturb the peace. He fondly recalled his cell in Wageningen's police station, which, he said, was infinitely more comfortable than his bunk in Spring Camp. As for the swill, there was no comparison. George's more scientific ruminations went over my head: his impassioned monologue on plant mutations; on the nutritional value of miscellaneous parts of the palm tree other than the coconut; on the fertility of the tropical soil, the history of the black tulip, and sundry exotic subjects of remote interest to me. Still, we seemed to complement each other in many other ways, and after the Japanese separated Frans from me, George became my best (and only) friend.

Eventually, even the Japanese guards supervising George's work found him useless for any type of labor. He was repeatedly sent back to camp. After about a week of being dragged out and sent back, he reached such a pitiful state that when a bed became available in our small sick bay, he was finally admitted. (Usually, the only way to get a bed in the sick bay was through the death of an occupant.)

In the bunk opposite me lived Henry. Although we now all carried more bone than flesh, Henry's body was somehow even more tentatively held together than most others'. His was an awkward frame of protruding ribs with matchstick arms and legs that called to mind a Giacometti sculpture. Henry was a very shy man, the loneliest of loners. He never initiated a conversation. When I asked him a question or expected him to respond to my greeting, he gave me a wordless sweet smile. Six months earlier, when most of us were still in good health, he told me that he had been called up as a member of the Dutch Army Reserve. In peacetime he had been the technical director of an ice-making factory. He was born and educated on Java and ten years older than I. Stationed in India as an aspiring cold-storage expert, he had converted to Hinduism. He became a fanatic vegetarian. It was not clear whether Henry followed the mainstream precepts of his newfound religion or belonged to one of its fringes; anyway, he only ate food that had fallen off a tree. Such strict adherence to a diet of tropical fruit had given him a skeletal appearance long before the Japanese further reduced his caloric intake. In the prison camps of the Indies and Singapore, where hardly any fruits and vegetables were available, Henry was compelled to break the sacred rules of his cult and take nourishment from a few grains of rice. Now, in our sick bay, white-haired and hunchbacked, Henry often made an effort to get out of his bed. For a moment he would stand next to his bunk, looking like a biblical apparition. Then he'd fall back. I never learned what his illness was, but he seemed to be dying happily, softly murmuring to himself. George said that he recognized the chant as a Hindi funeral hymn.

The days that I was allowed to stay in the camp on sick leave were extremely uneventful and monotonous. My few daytime companions were even weaker than I was. They were laid out flat on their backs, asleep or staring emptily into the distance. If I tried to talk to one of them, there was usually little or no response. Nor were there any books or old magazines for me to read. As so often before, I was very conscious of being the youngest. My fantasies were my only distractions. The other way I managed to keep utter boredom at bay was by focusing (even in the daytime) on killing the bedbugs, whose population had grown exponentially. I made sport of it — trying to kill two in one blow. I also kept score, counting the number of bugs I killed in one day and comparing it to the number killed during the day before. If I broke a previous record, I would feel a momentary pang of pleasure.

We were all weakening rapidly. There was little medicine, hardly any nourishment, and backbreaking forced labor. Some deteriorated slowly; for others death came quickly.

We became acquainted with death and familiar with its many faces. Some of the signs of approaching death were clearly visible: bodies covered with septic sores, arms and legs totally disfigured by a rash of pellagra (I saw one sore that had formed a circular hole a couple of inches in diameter). Scabies-type growths would also appear on scrotums and buttocks, and in groins and armpits. Gangrenous ulcers were among the worst horrors to watch — a spectacle of incurable misery. A sickening stench would accompany the crawling mass of rotten maggots gnawing at the open ulcers — a foul smell as sweet as, but a hundred times stronger than, that of a crunched bedbug. The distortions of beriberi were grotesque too: gross edema of feet and stomach, facial swelling, ulceration at the corners of the mouth, and an oversize raw scrotum. The withering dying seemed determined to prove the point that color is not always beautiful. It was as if they had been painted in the ugliest yellow fleshtone imaginable, mottled with streaks of lurid pink. A rainbow accompanied approaching death — blue, green, and purple.

Most deaths were from multiple causes. It was almost impossible (and in Spring Camp useless anyway) to pinpoint a single culprit. Men were afflicted with dysentery and, at the same time, with malaria. Or beriberi and diphtheria did them in, with a dose of mephitic tropical ulcers thrown in for good measure. To our doctors, and gradually to the rest of us, an exact scientific diagnosis was irrelevant.

We all suffered from one of two types of dysentery: bacterial or amoebic. We hoped and prayed for the bacterial kind, which was less fatal, in my case a mere harmless emptying of the bowels. My mates and I spent much time in the latrines comparing notes: those who saw blood in their stool were judged — and later usually proven — to be amoebic, and therefore in mortal danger. Death from dysentery, too, was unmistakable, a skeleton drowned in its own bodily waste.

Along the railroad malaria was by far the most widespread sickness. After the war it was established that malaria had been twice as common among POWs as all other illnesses combined.

This mosquito-borne disease could also be deadly. It also inspired us with black humor. The expression, "That Jap's got malaria on the brain," was much bandied about. This was when we considered the behavior of one of our guards especially peculiar or obnoxious. We also used the term to ridicule each other. In truth, there was nothing to laugh about: cerebral, or malignant tertiary (what doctors called "M.T."), malaria often meant a tormented struggle, ending in an inevitable and horrifying death. Its early symptoms were a violent flailing of the arms and legs, accompanied by wild outbursts of gibberish. At times the patient would be raging totally out of control, temporarily losing his capacity to think or act rationally. For some, cerebral malaria meant madness. Most POWs, including myself, were afflicted with a milder variety of malaria — the kind that only made us shiver with fever, hallucinate, and lose our stamina, aggravating our already weakened state.

We developed a sixth sense about what was happening to our bodies. Those who had the mental strength battled their illnesses; others denied it, and some just gave in. In the absence of any professional help from our impotent physicians, who were lucky if they were still in possession of their stethoscopes, we had developed an uncannily accurate capacity to diagnose ourselves. We had learned to do this by being in a group in which everybody was in a state of ill health and where a very thin line separated the living from the dead. We did not need any medical knowledge or training to understand that starvation led to dysentery, beriberi, and the other diseases. We knew how to identify the fatal cerebral strain of malaria. Each of us had a sense of whether he was going to die, or live.

The slowest forms of physical emasculation were the most painful to watch. Those stricken with beriberi or gangrenous limbs were more pitiful than the rest of us. At first we remained silent witnesses, listening helplessly to their moaning and their shrieks of pain. We had no palliative to give them, not even an aspirin. Later, when the place had become unbearably noisy, the moans and shrieks got on our frayed nerves. Losing our patience and compassion, we would yell at them to shut the hell up. Afterward, we would feel embarrassed and ashamed.

Strangely, though many died, it never occurred to me that I might die too. When others talked about death, I listened carefully but a little impatiently, not willing or able to visualize my own.

Besides George, a few other fellow POWs were part of a small circle of men with whom I communicated: Willem, a Dutch Eurasian; Colin, an Englishman, and Mac, a Scot. We spoke sparingly, for we were always too tired to engage in conversation. Very rarely, one of us would succeed in mustering enough energy to tell a joke — a feeble attempt at keeping up the morale. Usually the jokes were stale, as were the scenarios in which the tables were turned and we depicted for each other the Japanese suffering a worse fate than they inflicted on us. We imagined them all drowning simultaneously in the river or hanging from the very trees that we had to cut down for the railroad ties. As a way of venting our anger and frustration and keeping us mentally alert, it did not exactly work. We were too exhausted and demoralized to be lifted out of our gloom for more than a fleeting instant.

As the months wore on, each POW became more solitary; each individual tried to isolate himself from the pack. Our sore and diseased bodies required a lot. The only restorative we could muster was rest — we took scant interest in the complaints and self-pity of our mates. None of us could take much interest any longer in who, on any given day, might have been beaten up, collapsed, been sent to the sick bay, or died. In my waking moments, between trips to the latrines, I could only think of the food that I did not get and the life that I could not lead.

One night, lining up in front of our soup kitchen, where our rations were ladled by the cooks into porringers,

Mother at home in Scheveningen, 1935.

Father and Loet on the beach at Scheveningen, 1936. In the background is the old pier, now destroyed.

The Velmans family in Scheveningen, 1938. Mother (left), Loet (center), and Father (right).

Zeemans Hoop ("Seaman's Hope"), the coast guard vessel on which the Velmans fled Holland in May 1940.

Zeemans Hoop *manifest of ship's passengers and crew, May 1940.*

Mother and Loet (in uniform) in Indonesia, 1942.

Secret Wireless Room, Changi, 1943, *drawing by Ronald Searle. (Courtesy of Ronald Searle)*

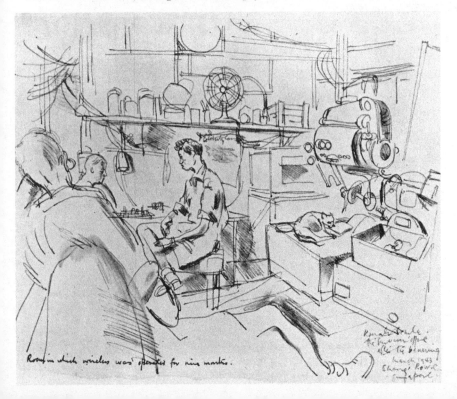

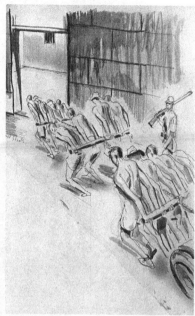

above left: Singapore, 1944, *drawing by Ronald Searle. (Courtesy of Ronald Searle)*
above right: Changi Gaol, Singapore, 1944, *drawing by Ronald Searle. (Courtesy of Ronald Searle)*

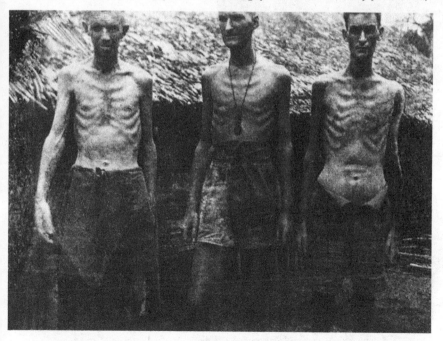

Prisoners whom the Japanese considered "fit to work." Note the prisoner on the right can't button his shorts because of his beriberi.

The Thailand-Burma "Railway of Death"; the railway cut through the rocks. *(Lex Noyon Collection)*

Typical huts for housing POWs. *(Lex Noyon Collection)*

Central Cemetery, Kanchanaburi. (Lex Noyon Collection)

Suspected Japanese war criminals, separated from the other prisoners, await transport. (Lex Noyon Collection)

Loet (left) *with two army buddies, Chaplain Chaim Nussbaum* (center) *and Eddie Rappaport* (right), *Singapore, 1945.*

Loet (right) *with Ambassador Yagi, chairman of the Hill and Knowlton Tokyo office* (standing to Loet's right), *the ambassador's wife* (seated to Loet's right), *and three senior managers of the Tokyo office.*

a murmuring protest quickly grew louder: the officers were having a gourmet supper. The Japanese did not give our own officers any special food privileges. We all shared the same meager rations. But that night they ate sardines! They had acquired the precious stuff from the villagers who lived farther down on the bank of the river Kwai and who used to climb up to the periphery of our camp to peddle and smuggle their black-market luxuries into our compound.

The Dutch and the British officers shared a hut, but remained each in their own half. It was a leaky rectangular bamboo structure, only a few hundred feet away from our own shelter but on the opposite side of the camp. We couldn't observe the sumptuous repast but could smell and taste the sardines in our imagination. It made us feel betrayed and angry. And it brought back all the old army's class and rank distinctions.

Earlier, the Japanese had ordered that all officers should work on the railroad like the common soldiers. The Dutch privates had loudly cheered the announcement; their British mates went on strike. The green eighteen-year-old conscripts felt outraged too that *their* officers were humiliated. But the protest only lasted less than a day. Our Japanese guards cut off all food supplies and threatened that more severe measures were in store. The British commandant ordered the men to abort the mutiny and get back to work.

I gradually got better. In the absence of Western medicines, we turned to natural remedies, and these helped my own rapid convalescence. Willem and one or two of the other Eurasians were quite knowledgeable about jungle vegetation. George, always prepared to demonstrate his academic expertise in tropical botany, assumed the role of supervisory consultant. It turned out that Willem and his friends needed no supervision; they possessed the practical skill that allowed them to distinguish the healing plants from their poisonous cousins. Once the medicinal plants were properly identified, they were cooked and eaten as a supplement to our meager meals. I believed in their healing power, and that faith may have been instrumental in my regaining some of my strength. There were also healthful delicacies to be found in the jungle: small tomatoes, coconuts (some of the Eurasians were nimble and expert tree climbers), unfamiliar kinds of peppers, figs, and spinach that grew hidden in the deepest jungle or in the most unlikely places, such as the cookhouse and next to the latrines. But all that could be gathered surreptitiously wasn't enough. It was a little bit of this and a little of that, never anything in sufficient quantity to satisfy the cravings of starvation.

As soon as I was a little more fit, and felt it, I was sent back to work again, clearing the railroad bed.

Statistics gathered after the war show that the Dutch POWs had a better survival rate than the Australians, who in turn did better than the British. One reason for the difference must have been the different cultural makeup of the three main groups of Western prisoners. The preponderance of men of Eurasian origin within the Dutch army accounted for the fact that the Dutch contingent, on the whole, had more survivors. Although most Dutch Eurasians were born and had lived in urban or developed agricultural areas, they proved themselves to be superior to the Europeans in adapting to the primitive life of the jungle. The Australians, many of them tough and hardened farmers from the outback, were in the best physical shape at the beginning of the war and also turned out to be the best organized and most disciplined. Despite the fact that they came across as rugged individualists compared to the Dutch and the British, they seemed less self-centered and genuinely keen to support each other. Many of the British were pale-skinned youngsters from Liverpool and other towns in the Midlands, just off the boat in Singapore, totally unprepared for the heat and humidity of the rain forest. Even though they were fairly young, they looked pale and undernourished even before they were taken prisoner. Many of them had little endurance.

There is not much point, of course, in making sweeping generalizations about national background. I realized this after the war, whenever I read published diaries or memoirs of ex-POWs that were, almost without exception, strongly biased in favor of the nationality of the author. However critical he might be of his own army, each writer tended to call the "others" undisciplined, egotistical, or just plain dirty. That is not to say that these generalizations did not carry a grain of truth. But the narrow national perspective of each individual POW always shone through. In documents found after the war, the Japanese commanders ranked the prisoners according to their endurance and usefulness. The Australians were given the highest mark; the British came second; the Americans third, and the Dutch placed bottom of the heap. There is, of course, some irony in the fact that, mainly due to the large number of Dutch Eurasians, the Dutch outranked all the others by far when it came to a category of no particular interest to the Japanese: that of survivor.

As for me, equally at home in different languages, accents, and mores, I was able to glide easily from one culture to the next and back again. My incubation as a chameleon had started in young adolescence and continued in camp. I was chummy with the Brits, the Scots, the Yanks, the Aussies, the Eurasians. The only nationality I did not feel any affinity to and stayed away from at all costs was the Japanese.

Throughout the monsoon season, walking anywhere — in our camp site and on the muddy trail to the railroad — was hard work, like running an obstacle course. It was difficult to keep from slipping and falling on the sopping wet ground. Next to cigarettes, boots were our greatest need — certainly more important even than food, for we had lost our appetites by now. (We rationalized this by telling ourselves that the dysentery had shrunk our stomachs so much that we could do without the food that we had no hope of obtaining anyway.) But the lack of footwear increased the risk of incurring an open wound, which could lead to infection and ulceration. One time, I remember, the Japanese supplied us with poorly made, shabby-looking tennis shoes. They weren't any help at all.

My work consisted of carrying rocks. Day after day Willem and I would make the same trip, dozens of times, each carrying a basket loaded with stones to the top of an embankment created by the dirt we had dug. There we would empty our load of stones, only to turn back for more. Late one afternoon, after we had been at it for more than a month, the guard who had been watching us, brandishing his bamboo stick and yelling "Speedo!" at me all day long, took it into his head to hit me in the small of my back, not with the stick he usually used but with a hammer. I fell down and blacked out. I was carried back to camp on a stretcher. The incident turned out to be a blessing in disguise. It was the last time I ever worked on the railway.

Our sick bay was restricted to twelve beds, at least nine of which were filled with dying men. The infirmary was now nothing more than a hospice for the dying. Terminally ill POWs for whom there was no room in the sick bay died on their own hard bamboo bunks. I was one of the few who, miraculously, survived that sick bay. After regaining consciousness, I was allowed to remain there for two full days. I enjoyed a luxurious rest. Instead of dragging myself out to the latrines, I was permitted the use of a bedpan.

On the third day the physician, a Dutch army doctor from Amsterdam, gave me a hard-boiled egg and discharged me.

"I'll assign you to the operating room," he said.

So, thanks to a fellow POW's sympathy, or compassion, I was appointed medical orderly. The medical staff consisted of one Dutch doctor, who was our resident general practitioner, and one traveling surgeon, who moved from camp to camp, plying his trade. Once every two or three weeks the surgeon, an Australian, would pay a visit to Spring Camp. It was our job to line up those patients who were considered likely candidates for amputation. Our surgeon stayed with us for a day or two and then went on his way again. In the operating room he was attended by two assistants. I was one out of that total of two completely inexperienced medical orderlies. My predecessor, a professional paramedic, had just died on the job. "Multiple diseases and exhaustion," my doctor said encouragingly when I asked about the cause of death.

The operating room was a small tent divided into two sections. One was the surgery proper, equipped with a wobbly bamboo operating table and a bucket that served as a receptacle for amputated limbs. A smaller table with a chair in front of it stood next to the operating table. When the surgeon arrived, he carefully put a few surgical instruments on the table. They consisted of a scalpel, a bone saw, and some bandages. The other half of the space was the recovery room, furnished with one bamboo bed, nothing else.

Our surgeon, tough, self-assured, but friendly, practiced only one procedure: amputating ulcerated and gangrenous arms, legs, and feet with his primitive saw, without anesthesia. As far as I can remember, I don't believe any of our patients survived their operation by more than a week or two. Yet the surgery was a marvel of precision, and the patient could now die with a clean-cut stump rather than an arm or leg bursting with pus, larvae, insects, and blood.

When I was not required to attend surgery, I worked in the sick bay or in one of the huts, scooping maggots out of open wounds and removing the white crawling larvae to a place where they could be burned. I also tried to scrub clean the bodies of the bedridden.

"Just leave my jockstrap alone," one of them said to me.

After every operation the other orderly — he was as weak as I was — and I would enlist any POW we could find in the vicinity to help carry the patient to the recovery room, where my colleague and I would bandage him. We would do this together, because more often than not we did not have the strength to get the job done on our own.

I am long haunted by the memory of the man we dropped because he was too heavy, or perhaps because we were too weak. Too often, my task was to wrap a spindly cadaver in burlap and help carry it to our jungle graveyard.

Funeral rites were minimal. Our primary concern was removing the bandages of the dead. These would then be boiled and reused. We improvised each new funeral service but kept it short. (A clergyman who had been with us at first had been sent on "up country.") Usually, the length of time we were permitted to spend at the graveside depended on the patience of the supervising guard. Most were in their usual hurry and made us perform this task, as any other, on the double. Others allowed us a few minutes of mourning and rest. On those occasions my mate and I would take a deep breath. It was our silent lament. As time went on, too many died in too quick a succession for the Japanese to bother with us too much. We were left alone and dared to stay at the cemetery for five or ten minutes. We would fetch a friend of the deceased or anybody who was able to muster enough strength to say a few words commemorating the short life of the soldier we were burying. Since everyone had to put in a full day's work on or along the rail bed, these brief services often took place at dusk, just before the evening meal. At one of these I remember that a young English lieutenant expressed his grief in the words of Rupert Brooke:

> If I should die, think only this of me:
> That there's some corner of a foreign field
> That is forever England . . .

Looking at the dense jungle surrounding us, I was struck by the aptness of those words, here at a burial ground some nine thousand miles from Flanders and twenty-five years after World War I.

It was impossible to determine which of George's many ailments ultimately caused his death, which had been as predictable as it was inevitable. He had been unconscious for a day, but became lucid just before his heart stopped. It was the middle of the night. I stood by his side for a long time, holding his hand. "I told you that it would do no good getting rid of my mustache," he whispered.

In the early days on the railroad, when we were building our huts and the access road, we had worked side by side. He was the only comrade with whom I once had a conversation about what it felt like to be humiliated, deprived, and degraded.

The next day I was not able to go back to work. I was sick with grief. There were so many memories of George. Under other, more normal circumstances, there would have been a proper funeral — not this bagging of the body and dropping it indifferently in a shallow rain-soaked ditch. Someone — myself perhaps — would have spoken of his courage, his concern for others, his help in identifying the edible plants that saved lives. Perhaps there would have been other reminiscences as well. Of his happy times as manager of a large tea plantation and of his student days at the agricultural university in Wageningen, Holland. And those of us who knew him might well have thought back to his difficult early youth on his father's plantation. He had adored his long-suffering mother and detested the autocratic father who, after the Sunday *rijsttafel,* would load his family into a horse and buggy and drive them to the house of his native Javanese concubine. While he was conducting his business in his mistress's bed, the family had to sit and wait in the carriage in the heat and humidity of the tropical afternoon.

But there was no time and little opportunity to mourn George. For a moment I lingered next to his grave. That day too I got drenched by the soaking rain. The earth of our cemetery was intersected by dozens of rivulets that had no place to go.

Mac, a Scot with a British stammer and a cheerful disposition, was the second of my circle to go. I don't recall all his exact maladies or symptoms, but they must have been similar to those of so many others who had sampled every entree on Spring Camp's menu of illnesses. Bodies riddled with diseases were slowly but steadily withering away. They would have made prize specimens at any research hospital. Beriberi had bloated stomachs and enlarged livers to elephantine proportions; knee joints were partially gone; arms and legs had lost most of their flesh, and what remained was eaten away, leaving a mass of gaping and stinking holes in which maggots were working away at the putrid remains of blood, sinews, and flesh. On top of that all, skin and eyes often used to turn yellow, the result of a catarrhal jaundice.

Victims of malignant tertiary malaria like Mac would drift from periods of complete lucidity into a phase of barking out statements that had a rational tone to them but bordered on madness, like "My potatoes are burnt," or "The sand on this beach is hot." Next would come a prolonged state of delirium — no words, only shrieks and cries, and then, shortly before the end, one single fierce and agonized howl. When it was one of my mates lying there, I did not dare to tear myself away from his bedside. I would stand there at his bedside, paralyzed, powerless, and sweating it out.

Mac was lucky: he was allowed to die in the sick bay, which also served as morgue and funeral chamber. Corpses passed through it quickly on their way to the graveyard. As the patients lay dying in the "recovery room" of our makeshift hospital, a little more attention was paid to them than to those who died in their own bunks in a hut deserted since the work parties had left it at the crack of dawn. Yet no one who entered the sick bay ever received more than minimal care. As much as the doctors and orderlies might have liked to give under other circumstances, there just wasn't enough compassion to go around. And as far as time and attention devoted to the dying by their healthier friends, there wasn't enough of that either. In his own attempt to survive, each man needed every precious free moment to look after his own body and his own state of mind. Each man remained wrapped in his own solitude. Exhaustion carried its own reward. Sick as we might be, at night we crept deep inside our own skins and sank into a bottomless sleep. I succeeded in getting deeper into my way of insulating myself from my illnesses and from my mates, burying myself in my small individual space. Instinctively, we felt that sleep was therapeutic; each of us tried to gulp it like a tonic.

We were too numb to consider suicide. When I walked through the hut of the dying, the emaciated arms stretched out to me were begging for water, medicine, a kind human gesture. All that anyone still on his feet could sometimes offer the near-dead was a crumb of rice, a wedge of cooked half-rotten fruit, half a mug of boiled water, or a wet rag to wipe off the sweat and the pus. No thought was ever given to a glass of hemlock or a final deadly injection. There was none of that: any wish to die had long since been dulled through pain and misery, and we had long run out of morphine or any other form of painkiller.

Death and illness tended to erase distinctions. In our graveyard bodies were indiscriminately dumped next to each other, without regard to rank or nationality. The sick bay was too small to accommodate the wishes of the dying. My colleague and I were too weak and indifferent to respond to a request by a dying Dutchman who wanted to be moved so that he could be next to a compatriot and old friend. We could not be bothered to drag a dying man out of his bed just a day or two before we would have to carry him to the graveyard anyway.

There was considerably more room in the regular hut

now because so many dead and dying had vacated their spots. It was now possible to trade places so friends of different nationalities could bunk next to one another. Only at the daily early-morning roll calls, which also served as the gathering point of the work parties, did we still stand at attention in our Dutch, British, and Australian units. But as soon as that was over, we intermingled freely for the rest of the day and went to sleep in whichever bunk we had selected. I had bunked between George and Mac. After they died, there were two empty spaces next to me.

After the war I learned that 41 percent of H-Force died while in camp or within a year or two after the war. We, for our part, weren't counting. Somewhat miraculously, over half of us were to survive, and I was to be one of that number.

Spring Camp was my school of death. It taught me that dying is the ultimate moment of loneliness. Well before their final spasms, my friends had detached themselves from the routine around them. Then I, the survivor, would live my own private moment of desolate loneliness.

Paradoxically, at each death the ties that bound me to those others who were still alive seemed to grow weaker. By this time the idea that friendship could bring a measure of comfort seemed ludicrous. No one could remember what it had been like to be well or how a friend's gesture or kind word might make one feel. Most of the time I lived as if I had no feelings left. I was doing my job as best as I could, but in a mood of utter detachment.

Only George's death interrupted my apathy. It made me feel even weaker than before, a feeling accompanied by a sense of real mental anguish. I do not recall whether my spell of despair following George's death lasted a day, a week, a month. But I have a memory of days passed in a mood of senseless survival and nights made restless by the realization that the next day would bring more of the same. Once I had lost my stamina, there was no further hope. My body was heavy with exhaustion, my mind empty. The images of earlier days, of Scheveningen, London, Bandung, and all that had taken place there — images that used to work on me like a tonic, that restored hope after a beating or some other gross humiliation, had gone. Whatever had been in my brain before had been emptied out. I felt no fear and no anger, only the most debilitating listlessness I had ever experienced. Fortunately, the depression (if that is what it was) did not last long.

The despair was gradually replaced by a determination: one way or another, I was going to beat the horrors of this living hell. I grimly decided that I was going to survive. To achieve this goal I decided on a tactic that I believed might work: I would take life one week at a time. From Sunday to Sunday. If I could just get through the week without a beating, a prolonged bout of malaria or other illness, I would have reached another milestone. I played my strategy as an exercise in self-discipline. Every Sunday I would make myself stand rigid in front of our hut. I would stay there for an hour, feet firmly planted in the mud, concentrating on how best to get through the next seven days — how I would chew my food carefully to press every vitamin out of it and into my system, how I would try to get as much sleep as possible to retain the maximum strength, how I would try to joke with and find stimulation in the company of my fellow prisoners. In other words, I tried to separate and then bring together the few positive elements of life in Spring Camp. Accomplishing a week's goal would get me to the next Sunday. And then we would see.

At mealtimes, I engaged in another mental game. With some imagination, my small unappetizing rations could be turned into a multi-course gourmet repast. The stringy and watery soup and the tiny portion of dirty gray rice were transformed into the smells and colors of the past: from Sundays with Father, white challah bread with aged Gouda; from my school days, open beef and liverwurst sandwiches for lunch, and for dinner, pea soup and steak swimming in melted butter; from my days of freedom in Jakarta, *nasi goreng* (fried rice with vegetables, shrimp, and meat) with plenty of *sate* (grilled chicken, pork, or lamb kebabs), or golden omelettes and pancakes with ginger for breakfast. I also recalled from my early POW days the recipes in my Yankee friends' magazines, especially the juicy steaks and all manner of mouthwatering sundaes and other ice cream concoctions. (I can still recall concentrating intensely on a sumptuous banana split.)

It may have been the sound of trumpeting elephants

that finally shook me out of my lethargy after George's death. The big beasts had been brought in to clear some trees that had fallen across the track after a particularly violent storm, making the service road almost completely inaccessible to vehicles. The elephants were the railroad's best friend. They were more reliable as workers than the prisoners; they could stand the heat and still remain healthy. The Japanese staff had worked out that the productivity of one elephant equaled that of eight men. The problem with the men was that so few were up to their task, and often they even had the nerve to die on the job.

The Japanese were hard on themselves too. I remember seeing armed infantry regiments with heavy backpacks, on their way to the Burma front, trudging by like medieval foot soldiers. They formed one long and silent line — an eerily soundless spectacle. They were either instructed not to talk or, more likely, simply exhausted. Behind them came the artillery pieces on long flatbed vehicles pulled by two or three dozen Japanese conscripts. An NCO walking alongside, carrying a whip with which he lashed out at any men who appeared to be dragging their feet. Another day it was a smaller contingent of Japanese, carting their belongings on wheelbarrows.

They looked healthy but tired. I wondered whether any of the Japanese soldiers ever fell ill — or whether they were allowed to be sick. After the war I came across a quote from a Japanese general who had assumed command in Thailand in mid-1943. It demonstrated that the

Japanese could not abide illness in the military. "Health follows will" was the holistic-sounding expression he used. "Lack of health is considered a most shameful deed," he continued. "Devotion until death is good."

By this time quite a number of our Japanese sentries had been replaced by Koreans who, having suffered for generations under Japan's colonial exploitation, were now eager to impress their Japanese employers with how cruelly they could treat the POWs.

Our guards, including the Koreans, had been keeping a pig in a cage. One evening we were ordered to attend a spectacle — the pig's execution. We were to be witnesses to some sort of sacrificial ritual, enacted like a game: our captors, shrieking with laughter, aimed their bayonets at the squealing animal, which ran from one end of its cage to the other. Finally, bleeding and exhausted, the pig sank to the ground, panting heavily. The coup de grace was delayed for one more round of jabs, aimed this time at its snout. Finally the pig, drowning in its own blood, whimpered and died. We went to sleep with the smell of pork barbecue in our nostrils. Not a scrap, not a bone, was thrown to us.

Although the calendar of 1943 — one humid month following upon the other — has blurred in my memory as a timeless stretch, I associate the ordeal of the pig with another story we heard, which was about humans. It must have happened around the same time. The shanghaied Asian workers were apparently suffering from the same diseases as the POWs, and in equally great numbers. The rumor was that the Japanese took pleasure in driving those Tamils, Malays, and Indonesians who were too feverish from malaria to work into the river Kwai, where they were forced to stand with the water coming up to their necks. With the guards joking about their generosity in allowing the slaves to cool off, some drowned right then and there; others who tried to crawl back ashore were shot.

One day we received a surprise visit: a Japanese field officer, unaccompanied by any guards or other military personnel, stopped by to visit. He spent more than an hour in our sick bay and entertained us with the story of his life. He had lived in America and conversed with us amiably in English. He described the San Francisco apartment in which he had lived with pride. It almost sounded as if he wanted us to share in his happy memories of the good old days in California. "I never had so much space," he said. He had no doubt as to the outcome of the war. "We are going to win," he said. Not once did he direct a question to us, but his monologue did pose an intriguing question: Was there a "different" and more humane type of Japanese? After he left I wondered whether he had noticed the sickly stench of our living, or dying, quarters. A few hours later he returned for a quick handshake. He did not speak, but left a large box filled with medicines for our dispensary.

Sometimes we had other Japanese visitors at the hospital. There were no adequate medical facilities for the Japanese in Spring Camp, or anywhere else in the neighborhood. Since health, according to Japanese military doctrine, seemed to be only a matter of self-discipline, they would come to our doctors for treatment, shyly and stealthily. They usually brought us only minor injuries needing attention — a dab of iodine (the only medicine amply available) for an open cut. The Japanese brought their own bandages, since we had none to spare. They showed us how stoical they were: the stinging iodine did not make them flinch. None of us ever saw any of our guards show any outward sign of pain or weakness.

Often, these patients sought out our doctors in the night. They were usually suffering from chronic gonorrhea and insisted on being injected with a yellow dye that was supposed to be a cure. The myth of the miracle dye seemed to have spread by word of mouth throughout the Japanese armies in Southeast Asia. Presumably started in Java, over the years it had been canonized as a cure for venereal disease. It was obvious that the gonorrhea patients felt they could not report their illness to their superiors.

Our doctors doubted the treatment would work. Their Japanese patients had a chronic condition, too far advanced for an easy cure. We were nonetheless prepared to cooperate. It gave us the opportunity to exercise a little leverage. In return for the shots, the Japanese would bring a couple of eggs or a small bottle of aspirin.

One day, in September 1944, a month or two before the completion of the new railroad, there was some unwonted excitement in the camp. We speculated what news had been signaled to our captors. Another victory, or similar bit of propaganda? Our guards had come running, gesticulating wildly. They finally made themselves understood: a train — the first one to make it through — was on its way. Then the first steam locomotive to reach Spring Camp promptly ran off the rails. Somehow the locomotive's wheels had left the tracks when it reached our sector, and the engine landed in the underbrush. We wondered whether it had been sabotage. We hoped that it was. This happened around noon. Within a few hours the elephants were back; a total mobilization was ordered. Not just every available POW, including officers and kitchen personnel, but also the Japanese daytime and nighttime sentries, the Japanese engineering unit, and the infantry units in transit — all were to report to the area where the locomotive lay toppled over in a ditch. By the time we got there, trucks had arrived, delivering large poles that were to be used to jack the locomotive back onto the tracks. Together, victors and vanquished put their shoulders to the task. For once, we were not supervised as closely as usual. A group of POWs assigned to hold the steel bars used to support two of the poles decided that now was the time to try a little sabotage of their own. They dropped their bars; the poles gave way, and the locomotive toppled back into the ditch.

A Japanese officer blamed a Thai elephant driver for the mishap and began beating him. Since the elephant driver was indispensable to the operation, however, he got off lightly. In the general disorder, our guards rained blows on our backs. But our morale was lifted by our success in delaying the completion of the railroad, if only by one hour. Our elation was short-lived; an hour or two later we learned that, a little farther down the road, an elephant had trampled a POW to death.

Over the next few weeks, trains fully loaded with men and supplies roared past Spring Camp; the railroad was nearly completed. We were apprehensive, fearing we might be taken farther up the line into Burma, where we had heard that cholera had nearly wiped out several encampments. We thought we might be assigned to work on the very last bit of the line, replacing the many POWs who had died there. To our relief, when the trucks came to fetch us, they carried us east, in the opposite direction, to Kanchanaburi, a large transit facility on the way back to Bangpong.

In the transit camp we found ourselves better off on several counts: we didn't have to work, food was slightly better and there was more of it, and there was music and theater. Furthermore, Kanchanaburi, an ancient walled city and the most populated area in this region of Thailand, was nearby. We went back to our old habits: smuggling was rife. Some of us still had some money left, since we had not been able to spend any in Spring Camp. While we could not hope to sell any of our clothes, which were in tatters, a blanket, a small shovel stolen in Spring Camp, a belt, and other similar items would fetch enough to buy a few pieces of fruit. It was a time of recovery, and the end of my career as a medical orderly.

At twenty I must have looked like one of the walking skeletons in the photographs of Bergen-Belsen or in the more recent television images of the starving Africans. But at least in Kanchanaburi we had no mirrors, and no vanity. Compared to some, I was well off. I was lucky to be alive.

My dysentery had cleared up; my malaria persisted. With the regularity of a menstrual cycle, the fever returned every four weeks. But luckily I was at an age when nature's recuperating powers are at their strongest. My mind was constantly racing, plotting short stories and the outline of a play, thinking about Mother and Father, my cousin Dick, and the rest of the family. Once again I would recall the taste and smells of my favorite foods: challah bread with sharp Gouda cheese, ginger *bolus*, strawberries and oranges, roast beef with mustard. When a friend gave me a banana, the rare taste of it made me hum with pleasure.

Even here, however, the Japanese guards seemed to get a kick out of beating and yelling at us. I never got used to it; the feeling of raw humiliation would come back every time. It was not so bad when the Japanese went on a rampage and beat up a whole group of us. Then we could collectively laugh off the whole incident and blow off steam by inventing new insults. But an individual beating was different — that really hurt.

One night in our Thailand camp we were discussing our captors, and wondering what kinds of jobs these people had held before the war. Where did they come from? we would ask ourselves. Since we knew nothing about Japan, we speculated that some of our guards might have been rickshaw-pulling coolies (like the ones I had seen in Singapore and on Java, even though those were of a different Asian origin). We speculated that our guards came from the lowest classes, reveling in finally being given the opportunity of getting their own back at somebody. Were they farmhands or policemen? We knew nothing about them — whether they came from Tokyo, a small town, or the countryside. Once or twice one of them, in a rare, slightly sentimental mood, told us about a wife, a child, or named a town or village that was home. From those spare confidences we drew the conclusion that our guardians had been selected at random for guard duty from the large pool of mobilized Japanese men. We Westerners finally reached a consensus: no matter what their background, these monsters were truly typical representatives of their nation as a whole. But how an entire nation could get its kicks from beating and torturing its prisoners was beyond us. It was as if each Japanese we encountered was a cog in a single monolithic wheel whose job it was to put us in our place. We should have known better than to oppose the emperor. Brutalizing us prisoners seemed to give the Japanese soldier an extra dimension of satisfaction. Sitting around and comparing my own emaciated arms and legs to the wasted bones of a half dozen of my mates, I got into a heated argument. Could there be any other side to the Japanese?

I asked. Were they hiding a facet of their characters that it was not in their interest to reveal to us? I was indignantly shouted down. It's their religion, we finally concluded bitterly. It's all about devotion to an emperor who is a god. But will change never come? I asked. Perhaps, one day, one of my friends said. But only when the country renounces its faith in its deity.

After a month or two in Kanchanaburi, we were shipped back to Singapore. On the day before our departure, we were ordered to participate in an elaborate ceremony celebrating the official inauguration of the railroad. We stood and watched the Japanese troops parading, cheering, and shouting. We marveled at a section in spotless uniforms who goose-stepped past their commanding officer. For our part, we received an extra ration of food and had to listen to a Japanese general as he extolled the virtues of his emperor. It was a fervent expression of faith. By now we had learned to recognize the import of such harangues — the Japanese wanted to demonstrate to us (scum of the earth) that their emperor was more than the symbol of the nation — he was a god, if not God himself. The completion of the railroad was the end of an important phase of the divine mission.

The speech over, we milled around. I had just left the line, where the POWs had received an additional festive bonus: a mug of weak tea and a tasteless piece of rice cake. I suddenly found myself face to face with the dapper little

Japanese guard who had used his hammer on me in Spring Camp.

He stopped. We glared at each other. It was unmistakably him, although he looked different — squeaky clean and all buttoned up in parade dress. For a moment I stood there with my mouth open, stunned. Then he started to bark at me: I was expected to salute. I shook myself and saluted him, correctly. He lingered for another moment. I saw him shrug, then he smiled and waved, bringing his own hand smartly to his cap. It all happened within a couple of seconds. Next thing I knew, he had vanished around a corner. I stood still, frozen in place for a while, staring after him. I fervently hoped that we would never meet again.

The zealous officer who speechified to us that day could not have foreseen the ironic fate in store for the Railway of Death. Almost immediately after its completion, the Allies launched intense bombing raids aimed at destroying the two main rail bridges. Soon the Allied air attacks wreaked so much havoc that when the Japanese finally withdrew from Burma, the railroad was practically useless in repatriating even the remnants of a severely beaten Japanese army on the run. But even before the bombs began to fall, the railroad proved a total strategic fiasco: the transport system turned out to be far less efficient than planned, able to provide only one-quarter of the daily supply requirements of the Burma front. After the war, Japanese military apologists tried to build a case that the railroad had met its goals. Yet even they admitted that the project could have been completed in a shorter time and with far less loss of life. In the end, the mammoth project turned out to have been a total waste of energy, at a cost of tens of thousands of lives, snuffed out in an ugly death devoid of all dignity.

6

Recovery

REPATRIATED TO SINGAPORE, we found that our destination was not Changi but Syme Road Jail, a small, colonial-era penitentiary composed of solid wooden huts.

The conditions in our new prison camp were naturally and infinitely better than those on the railroad. While our daily rations of rice and vegetables remained paltry, our diet was now supplemented by protein in a soup made of soybeans. We also received our first, and it turned out, our last Red Cross parcels, or rather half of one. Two prisoners had to share one box containing necessities and luxuries we had gone without for two years. I remember a can of Spam, a chocolate bar, some soup concentrate, and a cake of soap. It was only after our liberation that we were finally provided with an abundance of the boxes marked with a red cross.

I had suspected all along that the Japanese were helping themselves to the Red Cross supplies to which we were entitled under the Geneva Convention. My suspicions were confirmed after the war, when it was revealed that the Japanese had simply stolen the large supplies of food and medicines collected by the Allied governments and sent to the International Red Cross for distribution to the POWs throughout the Pacific region.

After our improved food rations — both in quantity and in quality — the most startling aspect of Syme Road was its cleanliness: the buildings were spotless. We could keep ourselves clean — we could wash, shower, and shave with clear water. There were proper latrines. Between dusk and blackout, electric lights could be switched on. To me, being able to read at night truly meant I was back in civilization.

A few days after our arrival, the Japanese officer in command addressed us, as customary. His harangue, however, differed from what we were used to. He shouted repeatedly, "Singapore Camp good!" implying that he was aware that conditions at the camps along the railroad had been below par. It sounded as if he was happy to see us back and felt a need to apologize for the bad treatment we had received in Thailand. I concluded that the end of the war must be in sight and that he wanted to distance himself from what had been going on along the Railway of Death. I also understood that he considered us his property — he, the Supremo or Japanese warlord of Singapore, owned everything and everybody on the island. He wished us to understand that he could not be held accountable for our treatment by his colleagues: we had been returned as damaged goods after having been loaned out temporarily. It was confirmed after the war that the general in command in Singapore had been at odds with the general in Thailand who supervised the construction of the railway. And I also learned that our Singapore general had been less charitable than I first assumed. His real motive for fattening us up was that he needed our manpower for his own construction projects in Singapore and that he did not want us to look too skeletal. The work to be done at the airport and in other locations required the POWs to walk through parts of town where the Chinese population would see us. There were already signs of unrest among the local population. It seemed therefore advisable to prevent any possible expression of sympathy for the emaciated POWs.

Syme Road had a regular season of theatrical performances. The Barn Theatre, staged in one of the barracks, featured productions of *Cinderella and the Magic Soya Bean* and *Rag Bag Revue* to great acclaim. Shows ran for five consecutive nights, followed by two or three days of rehearsals before the next offering opened.

Although there was at least one straight comedy, most of the productions featured stand-up comedians and female impersonators appearing in an entertaining number of cabaret sketches. Our actors were dressed in costumes ingeniously stitched together from rags and tent material. The decor, designed by the cartoonists Ronald Searle and George Sprod, always received an ovation. We greeted the many bawdy jokes and our lissome Eurasian transvestite with loud wolf whistles. Our female impersonator, having survived the railroad, had expanded his repertoire from the hula to the belly dance. At one of the first performances, attended by several Japanese officers, a samurai went backstage and ordered our feminine star to lift up his skirt. The officer, apparently a man of suspicious nature, wanted to make certain that no female had sneaked into the camp.

At the end of 1943 the news out of Europe was a little more encouraging — the invasion of Italy, the capture of Mussolini, and the reversal of Germany's fortunes at Stalingrad all lifted our spirits. By contrast, the slow pace of our military progress in the Pacific was agonizing. Though the Americans had managed to recapture Guadalcanal and the Solomon Islands, they were still a very long way from Singapore.

Several months later, in early May 1944, we were once again ordered to pack our belongings in a hurry. As I had worn out, lost, or sold everything that was not absolutely essential, my sole possessions consisted of one tin plate, a mug, a fork and spoon, a torn and patched mosquito net, one spare pair of socks and underpants, one tattered extra shirt, wooden clogs, and a small cake of soap (my treasured puttees had finally disintegrated). Our destination this time was not far, and its name had a familiar ring — Changi Gaol.

The prison of Changi was now bursting at the seams. More than 5,000 POWs were held in the old prison building, and another 12,000 in the encampment surrounding the jail. All were holdovers from various Singapore camps or recalled workers from the railroad. Many lived in makeshift huts, built around the central courtyard. Changi Square had grown into what could almost be seen as a homey, old-fashioned village green. The new huts that filled the courtyard had been cleverly constructed from rubber trees and bamboo poles, fastened together with barbed wire and covered in palm fronds. The men who stayed behind had applied their ingenuity and skills in a variety of other ways. They had planted small gardens; converted oil-fired water heaters for use with wood; fashioned showers out of pieces of stolen piping; concocted soap from palm oil and potash; tinkered together artificial limbs for the amputees out of wood and scrap metal; and tailored shorts and shirts out of tent canvas. The engraving machine that stamped "Rolex Waterproof" on the few remaining old metal watches was symbolic of how ingenious the POWs had become. The reconditioned timepieces fetched an exorbitant price on the black market.

If a stray dog or cat happened to wander into our prison, the poor animal would not last long. I recall one meal of roasted dog and of being furious when a group of old English friends from Syme Road failed to invite me to their repast of boiled cat.

With time to think, my thoughts returned to my parents. I envied my British and Australian mates because most of them had received at least one letter from home. Some mail from occupied Holland also managed to get through, via the Red Cross. But for some reason the Japanese were not allowing any communication to come through from the internees on Java. As time went on I was increasingly bothered by the lack of mail from the Dutch East Indies. When the others read their letters and postcards, I would watch them hungrily. Some held their letters close to their eyes, reading them over and over again. Just before leaving the port of Tandjong Priok for the crossing to Singapore, I had learned that Father and Mother were interned in a civilian camp near Jakarta. Since then we had lost all contact: there had been no news whatsoever about the fate of the civilians.

When I wasn't trying to bring back a picture from the past, I dreamed of the future.

I had fanciful ambitions and developed a scenario in which I would change the world. I had a vague notion about my own future career: in my last years at school I had thought about studying economics at the University of Rotterdam. But in prison camp it boosted my spirits to daydream about larger concepts: a better world and the abolishment of all armies. I fantasized about a political superstructure in which the Allies controlled life inside the borders of Germany and Japan. All German and Japanese military personnel would be sent to work in the factories and the fields of the countries they had occupied. They would become *our* prisoners and suffer a collective penalty for the harm they had inflicted. Each year a new generation of eighteen-year-old Germans and Japanese would be drafted and sent far away from home. I wanted to see them pay. As for the Japanese, I wanted us to prove that our cultures were poles apart. The price we would extract as punishment would be high, yet our conduct would always remain humane and fundamentally more honorable and compassionate than their treatment of us had been.

In my dreams I saw Churchill and Roosevelt at the moment of victory declare all wars abolished and all weapons banned. With unanimous approval all nations would stop the silly game of dressing their men up in uniform and pinning rows of medals on their chests. My dream world was gloriously utopic. Yet in mapping it out, I always retained a small empty reservoir in the back of my mind. It was as if I did not wish the dream to be complete. I needed to be able to look forward to doing more fine-tuning, to think through every detail, to sort out every option of how to deal with our defeated foes so that they could never become a tyrannical threat to their neighbors again.

Changi too had a theater, the Coconut Grove, with its own female impersonator, billed as "Judy Garland." It is hardly surprising that in many reports of POW survival, one factor is often overlooked: wit, humor, and the capacity to laugh were indispensable to survival. Often the most miserable looking Tommies and the most misanthropic intellectuals would turn out to be the funniest men in the camp. To stay alive it helped, of course, not to contract a deadly disease and to stay far away from the places where cholera was rampant; but the joke, the quip, and the funny sketch all worked like powerful tonics. They played a key part in the pursuit of survival.

By the time I returned from the railroad, my original circle of friends had evaporated. Almost all my old buddies from Java, from the Flying Dutchman canteen, and from Spring Camp had died on the railroad. I had outlived George, the gloomy botanist who had become my *slaapie* and who had died of multiple ailments; Frans, the bartender with the irresistible grin, who had been beaten to a pulp and contracted amoebic dysentery early on; Mac, raging with malaria-induced dementia at the end; and Colin, the Englishman. Colin had been the last of our group to go, swollen with edema, clutching a picture of his wife and child. Only Willem, the Dutch Eurasian, with his vast and indispensable knowledge of jungle vegetation, and I, the group's wiry Benjamin, were left.

Working on the railroad had brought officers and rank and file a little closer together. In Spring Camp, joint work parties had included Dutch lieutenants and captains. Their laboring alongside enlisted men had boosted everyone's morale. (By contrast, the British officers had not shared in the workload. In some camps, including Spring Camp, the Japanese had excused them from hard labor, although in other camps the Japanese, who had never signed the Geneva Convention, compelled all officers to participate in hard labor) Generally, the rank and file perceived that in Thailand and Burma the officers had been treated badly too. They too had been treated like slaves. They too had been beaten, punched, and kicked; no one had received meaningful preferential treatment. Although in Singapore, under better conditions, some measure of discipline was restored, we never again regarded our officers in quite the same hostile light as before our joint ordeal on the railroad.

Changi was well run, in large part because the Japanese kept themselves in the background, although they sometimes looked in at our theatricals and Sunday services. These services were generally well attended, for Changi had an active religious life. For many POWs, to go to church was also a convenient excuse not to have to join a Sunday work party.

Out of curiosity and in spite of my avowed agnosticism, I had started attending Jewish services conducted by Chaim Nussbaum, a Dutch Orthodox Jew who spoke both Dutch and English with a slight Yiddish accent and who was an ordained rabbi. Nussbaum was a broadly educated and self-taught intellectual: he held a doctorate in physics and had a profound knowledge of philosophy. Charismatic and gutsy, he had gathered together a group of British, Australian, and Dutch Jews, who had knitted themselves into a tight family, despite the differences in language, nationality, background, and profession. We counted among us a dentist, a copywriter, a jeweler, a corporate executive, a traveling salesman, and a lawyer who was to become a prime minister of Malaya after the war.

Being a secular Jew, I was the only member of Nussbaum's circle who failed to comprehend the significance of Nussbaum's strictly orthodox observance of the Sabbath and holiday rituals. But I experienced a new sensation: the warm feeling of belonging to a community.

I shared a prison cell built for one person with Chaim Nussbaum and a third cellmate, a young Dutch Gentile named Lex who had fallen seriously ill on the railroad with several jungle diseases. Chaim lorded it over us, since he was enthroned on the elevated concrete slab in the center of the cell that was the only bed. Lex and I lay on the floor on either side of Nussbaum's perch. Although it was cramped, we had so few possessions that we managed not to be too much in each other's way. Going to the latrines at night was another matter. Three men now occupied our dungeon, designed for the housing of one prisoner. And other prisoners had installed themselves in the corridor outside our cell. It was hazardous going. I would often stumble and sometimes fall over some prone emaciated body in the dark, causing him to wake up and curse me for my clumsiness. Everyone in our cell block was suffering from at least one illness, and we were all seriously undernourished. And yet we were the strong ones — the ones who had survived so far.

Lex came to some of Chaim's lectures on Judaism, which were attended by a number of other interested non-Jews. He was an easygoing, pleasant, shy-mannered, unpretentious intellectual. Artistically talented, he had a strong sense of social responsibility. He showed little interest in the mundane aspects of our prison existence, but he would wax enthusiastic about Mozart, his life's great love. He also worried that he might not regain the strength to play the piano again. Fifty years later, when Lex and I finally found each other again in Amsterdam, he had retired as a highly respected professor of social work. He wistfully recalled his dream of becoming a professional pianist, which had been torpedoed by the war. He also told me about the POW memories that would haunt him for the rest of his life. One day, in a POW camp on Java — one that I had the good fortune to miss — his camp commandant had ordered Lex to kneel before him. With all the other prisoners looking on, the commandant had drawn his sword and laid it across Lex's clean-shorn skull and neck, moving it back and forth in a sawing motion. Lex had no idea why he had been singled out. He held himself rigid, sensing intuitively that the slightest move on his part would provoke the blow that would decapitate him. Nothing happened. After what seemed an eternity, Lex was allowed to rejoin the ranks. Half a century later, he still had no clue what it was that the Japanese officer had in mind. Nor did he understand what he had done to deserve the deadly game that had been played with him. Lex also witnessed an execution similar to others that occurred in several camps in the early days of our imprisonment on Java. It was in Lex's camp that three Eurasian soldiers had crept under the barbed wire, night after night, to visit their wives or girlfriends, returning in the same way the next morning before daybreak. During several weeks, the Japanese guards observed and good-naturedly tolerated these nightly excursions — until the day the Japanese camp commander changed his mind or received an order to impose a stricter regimen. The three lovers were bayoneted to death against the barbed wire. Lex had stood nearby, in the front row.

Everything being relative, that second stint in Changi was not an unhappy period for me. It became a time of creative overdrive. Several handwritten magazines were making the rounds in the camp. Nussbaum decided to try his hand at one, and I became its editor. We called it *Habeemah: The Changi Jewish Forum*. I translated articles by Nussbaum and others from Dutch into English, wrote a short story, and edited and typed the lot onto the back of recycled prison records. Several budding cartoonists from Holland, Britain, and Australia — among them Ronald Searle and George Sprod, neither of them Jewish, both of them destined for fame after the war — supplied the illustrations.

Searle and Sprod were our Tweedledum and Tweedle-dee: both spent the whole day sketching; both were extremely talented; both had a dry sense of humor and, of course, both were extremely thin — as we all were.

Habeemah was not the only camp magazine. The *Exile* was Changi's general circulation vehicle — one copy was available for distribution among a potential audience of more than 10,000. It was a miracle that Ronald Searle and his fellow editors managed to put out no less than ten editions of the magazine within a period of six months.

The one and only copy of *Habeemah* was widely circulated: besides the fifteen-odd members of our Jewish congregation, many others were interested in it as well, for everybody was famished for reading material.

Moishe (called Mose), a Dutchman and member of the small coterie surrounding Nussbaum, cut a curious figure. He was tall, stooped, and thin as a reed. His most striking feature was his big nose. A salesman representing a Dutch kitchenware company, he had been on his first visit to the Indies when he was stranded there by the German occupation of Holland. In the Jewish congregation, he functioned as Nussbaum's hyperactive acolyte, assisting in the preparation for religious services, carrying books and refreshments from the canteen to patients in our sick bay, and ferrying messages between Nussbaum and the command staff. He was a bachelor and acted like an old spinster. He was also a natural caregiver. In a parental frame of mind, he had selected me as one of the favorite targets of his beneficence. That was after he had taken care of Nussbaum. First and foremost he wanted "Nuss," as he called him, to get the best of whatever he could scrounge: a spoonful of extra rice, a piece of fruit, some stringy vegetables. Most of this could only have come out of his own rations. Although he sometimes seemed to be trying to starve himself to death, his cheerful mien and darting eyes contradicted any such intention. When Nuss was busy — and he usually was, looking after his flock — Mose loped after me, begging me to send him on an errand or to let him wash my threadbare clothing. I firmly rejected his largesse, but Mose kept pushing. If I had not adamantly declined his offers, he would have tried to force all of his own food down my throat. One evening I found him in one of the best seats of our makeshift theater. He had been reserving it for me since late that afternoon and left the theater immediately after he had forced me to occupy it. That day I asked myself the question that had occurred to me before: Had Mose turned into this groveling altruist as a result of his imprisonment and time on the railroad? Or was this simply his fundamental character?

In Changi, as the months passed, Mose grew into an increasingly lonely figure. He wandered about on his own, muttering to himself. He had amassed a heap of old prison records from the stock of sheets that also served as cigarette paper and for the printing of camp magazines. In the evenings he sat hunched on his bunk, scribbling furiously. "I am writing everything down for Joshua, my only heir," he said.

Sitting around in the evening, drinking mugs of weak tea, my friends and I would discuss literature, religion, and politics. I was like a sponge, in a frenzy to learn — through books, the knowledge of my friends, and the exchange of ideas. My pet subject, on which I held a strong and strictly uninformed opinion, was the political structuring of the postwar world. I was still playing with ideas of how to reorganize the postwar world. I would draw diagrams of a new League of Nations, but always with the proviso that the victorious Allies would lord it over the Germans, Italians, and Japanese for a long time to come.

I didn't quite realize this at the time, but if prison camp was a microcosm of the Western world, there was not much hope for international cooperation. As a general rule, the Australians, the Americans (a small minority), the British, and the Dutch behaved as if they hated each other's guts. Where the different nationalities shared kitchens and medical facilities, the rules of national nepotism always came into play. Cooks and medical orderlies were appointed based on the nationality of the ranking POW officer. Further substrata existed. Among the British there were the Scots, the Irish, and the genuine limeys. The Dutch contingent consisted of the Eurasians and a small group of whites who, following the short-lived integration brought about by the misery of the railroad, once again kept themselves aloof from their fellow POWs of mixed Dutch/Indonesian blood. Further divisions along class lines inevitably reasserted themselves, pitting rank and file against officers. The camaraderie that had prevailed on the railroad was forgotten. Especially disliked were those British officers who carried their swagger sticks with renewed pride.

I was the exception, I suppose. Like a chameleon, I found myself drifting easily from one ethnic group to another, and felt at home pretty much everywhere.

In Changi the Japanese paid each POW a pittance. Since the Japanese neither subscribed to nor believed in the Geneva Convention, we assumed that our remuneration followed some Japanese military pay scale, although our pay must have amounted to only a fraction of the minimal wage earned by the Japanese soldiers. A small percentage was taken off the top of our meager earnings by our own internal POW administration for the purchase of supplementary food supplies and medicines. Chaim Nussbaum's congregation also collected voluntary contributions. In the Singapore camps there was always some cash on hand. I myself had been able to conceal a few banknotes left over from my black-market days. Surrender to the Japanese had not entailed surrendering regimental money reserves; cash had been as cleverly concealed as radio parts. Whenever I could find the luxury of a coconut or a cake of soap, I shared it with Lex, who in his weakened state was not capable of fending for himself. As always in life, money remained a fundamentally indispensable commodity, even within the enforced confines of our captivity.

Our leisure came to an abrupt end when the Japanese decided to use the POWs for a major new construction project to enlarge the Changi airfield. Once again, we were being shown how expendable we were; nothing was done to make the work efficient or bearable. It seemed as if the bad times had returned. The only redeeming, yet dangerous, feature of our forced labor was that, once again, it offered some of our most daring and ingenious pilferers the opportunity to purloin tools, lightbulbs, canvas, Japanese rations, and whatever else they could lay their hands on. Although I was not selected for the outside work parties, I was put to work, without a break, on repair and maintenance jobs inside our barracks.

The inevitable happened. An Australian was caught red-handed and was beaten almost to death. The excitement of being back in Changi had worn off, especially now that the Japanese had started to reduce our rations again. In the Japanese view, the less we were given to eat, the harder we would work. Our guards seemed convinced that the lack of a few more scraps of food would make us stronger and restore our health. They administered this message with enthusiastic beatings.

The reduction in our rations was accompanied, almost simultaneously, by a sudden clamp-down on all entertainment. The Coconut Grove had become an integral part of our lives. The anticipation of distraction through laughter, the excitement of the performances themselves, and their relaxed aftermath — all brought a lift to our morale that could last for days. When they closed down our theater, the Japanese administered a massive dose of communal depression by depriving us of a form of nourishment that we needed just as badly as food.

The censorship was not directly related to the thievery. It started because of a song composed and performed by my favorite entertainer, Bill Williams, a British singer who accompanied himself on the piano. Williams had a magnetic hold on his audience of emaciated youngsters when he sang "There'll Be Blue Birds over the White Cliffs of Dover" or "A Nightingale Sang in Leicester Square." I used to hum those songs for days afterward. And I would daydream how after the war I would turn into a Maurice Chevalier–type boulevardier and sing my way through life.

The song that gave the Japanese offense was entitled "On Our Return" and was a roaring sentimental success. Its meaning was obvious — we were going home. One night a Japanese general and his staff were in the audience. They were evidently not amused. The place was shut down for good.

I was convinced, as I had been many times before, that the war was about to end. The Allies would invade continental Europe, the Americans would invade Japan, and the British would recapture Singapore. In May 1945 we celebrated the defeat of the Nazis. Perhaps we were better informed than our Japanese guards; in any event, there wasn't the slightest change in the way they went about demonstrating their contempt for us. I know now that our senior officers were more worried than I was (in my naïveté) about what might happen to us when the Allies got around to launching an invasion in our part of the world. But I did join in the speculation. Would our captors massacre us all? What else could we expect? Who could second-guess these people who didn't seem to be tired of war, not even after fifteen years?

It became difficult to communicate with Mose, who desired increasingly to be left alone. For most of the day he could now be found seated on his bunk, hunched over his writing. As the weeks passed, his eyes no longer glittered; they had turned dull. Every so often he became his old self again, intent on looking after Nuss and me. Yet his enthusiasm had slackened. "There is so much to write," he said. "I must leave instructions before it is too late."

7

Renascence

WE HEARD ABOUT HIROSHIMA ON AUGUST 7, the day after
the A-bomb blast. We did not understand exactly what had
happened, but we were convinced that it would speed up
our deliverance. We shouted our joy like corks popping out
of a bottle. I have a clear memory of Nussbaum leaning
against the western wall of our cell, facing toward Jeru-
salem, chanting and banging his head softly against solid
cement. His small, shrunken figure gently rocked back and
forth, head and shoulders covered by his oversize prayer
shawl. The Japanese acted as if nothing had happened.

The next day they were gone. Was it a trap? We did
not dare venture outside the perimeter of our jail. Twenty-
four hours later the guards were back again. But this time
they were carrying small sidearms only; they had left their
rifles and bayonets behind. Meanwhile, Allied planes were
dropping leaflets on us, advising us to remain put until the

arrival of the British troops. Throughout the first week of our suspended liberation our mood swung wildly from euphoria to fear, from hysterical laughter to tearful prayer.

During those first tense days — from the moment the first bomb fell on Hiroshima until the day Japan surrendered — we remained cooped up. We watched our guards anxiously. They no longer took roll call, but nothing else in our daily routine changed. Yet we could not stop celebrating: we slapped each other on the back, shook hands over and over, cheered each other on, and broke into song. It was a bit of an anticlimax when we were finally told that the war had officially ended. We hadn't been very good at handling so much tension. Occasionally, we lost our cool. The news that the war was truly over took time to sink in.

The Japanese surrender was on August 15, 1945. It was only later that I learned that the Japanese general in charge of our part of Southeast Asia, headquartered in Saigon, had been ready to disregard his emperor's orders and to defend every inch of territory under his command to the bitter end. When he had refused to lay down arms, the emperor's brother flew from Tokyo to Saigon to enforce Hirohito's order to surrender. If he had not done so, an order to kill all POWs would have remained in effect. Clear instructions had been issued: all POWs were to be massacred on the day the first Allied soldier set foot on any spot of land that was under control of the Saigon command. The Allies, for their part, also had a firm timetable:

an invasion north of Singapore had been ordered and was scheduled for early September. Fortunately for us, Japan's capitulation came just in time, a month before we would likely all have been killed. This was my last lucky escape.

By the end of August, the Kempetai — the previously dreaded military police — had replaced our regular guards. Suddenly, the Japanese were on their best behavior — they treated us well, almost obsequiously. Suddenly Red Cross parcels arrived by the truckloads. On August 30, the first British troops landed, and we were visited by medical units that established radio contact with their headquarters offshore. The next day British bombers flew over the Changi area and dropped canisters containing food supplies, vitamin pills, Ovaltine, and cigarettes. We cheered each parachute as it came down. The Kempetai were ordered to surrender their sidearms. They were now only armed with homemade wooden toy rifles. They looked ridiculous. But we were still too browbeaten to take revenge or demonstrate our anger. We had other things on our minds: how to get in touch with parents, wives, children, and girlfriends. I remember watching a lone English ex-POW giving a Japanese guard a piece of his mind. He was standing nose to nose with his foe and was screaming with fury. I looked on with indifference. There was no visible reaction from the Japanese soldier either.

We were told that we would each be allowed to send one telegram to our loved ones. I thought long and hard about how to word my one precious missive to my parents. We compared notes among ourselves. A Dutch architect who had worked with the team that designed the Dutch pavilion at New York's 1939 World's Fair wired one single sentence to his young bride: "Still studying the gentle art of becoming a better husband." That message had a nice ring to it. I have always kept it in mind.

The Kempetai remained on guard outside our gate. Whoever issued their orders must have been under the mistaken impression that we needed protection from the native population. The people of Singapore, however, seemed solidly on our side. Small groups of native Chinese came up to our gate, smiling and waving. When we ventured outside the camp, walking along the perimeter fence, they cheered and threw fruit and other edibles in our direction.

The newly arrived British troops assigned to our welfare wore armbands with the letters RAPWI (Recovery Allied POWs and Internees). A Dutch delegation, wearing the same insignia, arrived to look after the 2,000 Dutch ex-POWs in Singapore.

One day, Willem and I got a lift out of Changi. A British officer drove us in his jeep to the busy port. We strolled along the docks to watch the British warships at anchor and the hustle and bustle on deck. A naval officer invited us aboard his warship. We were led to the mess, where we gorged ourselves on tea with a generous quantity of milk and sugar, and white bread thickly spread with butter and marmalade — delicacies that we had neither seen nor tasted for years. I promptly threw it all back up.

The next day, back in Changi, Willem and I baked a cake from a special festive ration that had been distributed to each inmate: half a dozen eggs, a few spoonfuls of flour, and lots of sugar. An unusual recipe that resulted in a surprisingly delicious cake — but we couldn't keep that down either.

The Kempetai guards posted outside our barracks stood at attention all the time. They saluted us when we passed through the gates. We ignored them. Then, one day, they too were gone, as if they had evaporated into thin air.

In the liberated camp, our euphoria reached its zenith when Admiral Mountbatten, commander in chief of the Allied forces in Southeast Asia, came for a visit and stepped up on a wooden soapbox just inside the main gate. Dressed in an immaculate white uniform, he gave a charismatic performance, praising our (presumed) courage and assuring us that the world would forget neither our suffering nor the atrocities committed by the Japanese. We cheered and whistled and felt good about ourselves. For a moment, I relaxed the wariness and suspicion that had become my second nature. I had learned from bitter experience to take statements and promises made by military authorities with more than a few grains of salt. Mine was a deep-seated cynicism, a POW mentality that, once acquired, would never wear off. It made each setback and each disappointment easier to accept. After all, what was so bad about the unfulfilled promise, the unscotched rumor, the hypocritical pep talk? In the end there was only one reality: death. Death was the ultimate broken promise.

Yet even for the toughest of survivors, there were times when we could not help but let our guard down. I was anything but tough and unemotional when I first heard about the Nazi extermination camps. One of the first British officers flown in from Australia turned out to be a Jew who, at a gathering of the Nussbaum congregation, told us about the death camps of Europe and the execution and extermination of millions. We, who had considered ourselves hardened veterans and who thought that we had seen and lived through the worst, had great difficulty controlling our emotions. Most could not hold back their tears.

I was unable to cry. I wanted to, but could not. Instead a storm of anger raged inside me. After a day or two the fury calmed down. I was left with a dull sense of mourning. At that Friday night's services, Nussbaum's liturgical lamentations tore at my heart. I still did not understand the Hebrew text, but I recognized that his wailing had now acquired an additional contemporary meaning. A horrifying one at that: chants both grave and relevant, and deeply disturbing. My attention wandered to my grandparents and their little rooms in the walk-up on the Rechtboomsloot. I saw the whole family before me. Although all four of my grandparents had died a natural death before the war, theirs was the community that had brought forth my aunts, uncles, and nieces, who were likely to have perished.

Only a few weeks later, the Holocaust had already become an abstract and remote concept to me. I simply refused to allow it to penetrate my thoughts, fearful that it would overwhelm me. I shut the dead of Europe, like the dead of Asia, out of my life. I did not know how to mourn — not even my own relatives and the school friends I had left behind in Scheveningen, most of whom, I felt certain, must have been murdered.

There was one eye-opening moment of truth for me, which I managed to sweep under the carpet almost immediately. Shortly after receiving the first news from Europe, I told one of our liberators, an English Jew in captain's uniform, that I had escaped from Holland before ending up on the railroad. He frowned. "Well, then, poor sod, you missed a double whammy," he said. Much later, I realized that, bad as Spring Camp and my whole period of imprisonment had been, it had saved me from Auschwitz.

One Friday evening in Changi, on my way to have a chat with Nussbaum, I passed Mose, who had found a table to write on more comfortably. "No one in my family has survived," he said mournfully. "I know it. I feel it in my bones. None of us here has been told what has happened to our families. I am the first of all of you who knows." He turned away from me. "Now I have to write it down for Joshua." It took me a moment before I grasped the meaning of his biblical allusion.

I had received word that my parents were alive, in a civilian prison camp in Jakarta. Chaim Nussbaum was given a pass to fly to Jakarta to be reunited with his wife and three children. He was only granted a few days' leave but went out of his way to hand-deliver a long letter from me to my parents. The news he brought back was grim. The Dutch civilian population had taken its share of suffering. At the time of liberation, they too were near the point of starvation, and had been cowed, beaten, and tortured. Theirs had been three years of tough and pitiless internment. (Some 15 percent of all civilian internees had perished.)

Once I got used to my newfound freedom, I became bored with the life of a liberated prisoner of war. I felt stifled and restless. There was a new life to be lived somewhere out there. I found the daily routine dreary: a relaxed early-morning roll call, followed by a leisurely breakfast; a little later, a nourishing lunch, topped off by a splendidly elaborate high tea (at least, that was the way food tasted to us after three years of the monotony of our Japanese diet). The problem was how to fill the hours between mealtimes. Of course, there was always chess or bridge to fall back on, but to me, games now seemed a flight from reality — challenging and enjoyable only when one was a prisoner living behind a bamboo fence. We were free to take a stroll around the neighborhood, or take a nap at any time. But the novelty and luxury of so much leisure time soon wore off. The emptiness of our evenings was taken up with wishful speculation about our chances for a speedy repatriation to Holland — or, at least for me, the less welcome prospect of being pressed into active military service in Indonesia, where renewed civil unrest threatened to escalate into a full-scale uprising against colonial rule.

After about a month of this, I decided that I'd had enough of military life and walked out the gate of Changi. On strictly legal grounds I was a deserter. Under normal circumstances I would have been in serious trouble. Fortunately for me, our administration was in such disarray that I felt reasonably confident that going AWOL carried little risk. Not only did my departure from the barracks lead to no negative consequences, it didn't seem to have been noticed at all. It never crossed my mind that I could have been arrested, thrown into jail, and court-martialed.

The escape from my military straitjacket proved to be well worth it. I could breathe freely and be myself again in ways that were impossible in the army. It felt good to return to being a happy-go-lucky adolescent. From now on, I felt, things would be looking up. I craved new adventures. I walked into what looked like an empty office building and found myself a rent-free room with a bed in it. A Chinese porter told me that, during the Japanese occupation, one floor of the building had been the sleeping quarters of a select caste of high-ranking Japanese officers. The rest of the building had been used for storage. Now that the Japanese were gone, it was an ideal place for me to live. A few other "deserters" joined me. We used a small communal kitchen. The building was on the docks and owned by KPM, a Dutch shipping company that had not yet resumed its Singapore operations or reclaimed its building.

I immediately struck up an acquaintance with two of my neighbors, both Hungarian émigrés, serving as doctors in the British army as members of the liberating forces. They had discovered the KPM building on the day that I moved in.

I also found myself a job. Among our liberators was a Mr. Aardewerk, a man about ten years my senior. True to my Dutch upbringing, it never occurred to me to address him by his first name. Mr. Aardewerk was a Dutch army information officer and a Jew. Before the war he had lived in Antwerp, where he had been the publisher of a magazine. When he heard of my interest in journalism, he invited me to accompany him to the offices and printing plant of the *Straits Times*, Singapore's leading newspaper. There we met the editor of *SEAC*, the daily paper named for the British South East Asia Command, which it served. The editor was a hard-drinking Fleet Street veteran who readily agreed that the Dutch, too, were entitled to have their own daily newspaper and invited us to share his presses as well as his premises. He was less generous with the bottle of Scotch on his desk. We named our paper *Oranje* (orange being the Dutch national color, in honor of the House of Orange, the royal family). Aardewerk appointed me deputy editor — an important-sounding title that compensated for the fact that the entire editorial staff consisted of the editor (Aardewerk) and myself.

I enjoyed the work — translating into Dutch the international news and features carried by our British sister publication. I learned to do layouts, and was given the job of broadcasting news bulletins on Singapore Radio aimed at the liberated Dutch in Indonesia. I also wrote up for *Oranje* the news reports that we received from the wire services' correspondents on Java. The news from there was not very reassuring. We feared for our families and did not relish the likelihood that we would soon be reoutfitted, rearmed, and repatriated over there to battle the Indonesian insurgents. In some of Java's major cities, armed local gangs had taken hostages and killed Dutch civilians. In the power vacuum created after the Japanese capitulation, law and order had vanished, and chaos was rife.

I soon forgot I had ever been hungry. I didn't even take notice of the fact that I belonged to the ranks of the well-fed once more. Apart from the unshakable bouts of malaria, the only thing that made me suffer was the heat. In Spring Camp and all along the railroad I had become inured to the tropical climate. Now, back in civilized clothes (and still living in a pre-air-conditioning era), the sweat dripped from my forehead into my neck and soaked my armpits.

The Dutch government, back in Holland after five years of exile in England, was determined to reestablish its control over its colonies. Few Dutch politicians had the foresight to understand that European colonialism was at an end. Neither the government nor the public was prepared to relinquish its most precious possession. We insisted, as a nation, on reclaiming our patrimony. Meanwhile a small but vocal group of Indonesian politicians, headed by Sukarno, a skilled and opportunistic demagogue, declared independence and founded the Republic of Indonesia. This historic event took place on August 17, 1945, two days after Japan's surrender. The Dutch authorities, having only limited military resources and manpower at their disposal, were eager to press all liberated POWs into service, despite their less-than-sturdy physical condition. The former prisoners would be a useful addition to new contingents of Dutch soldiers arriving from Britain, Australia, and the home country. The POWs were seen as experienced, well-disciplined veterans who would form the backbone of an army that would put the ragtag bands of Indonesian rebels in their place. The Indonesians, viewed by the Dutch as a bunch of ungrateful traitors, were holding a tidy arsenal of weaponry left behind by the Japanese.

Even if it meant going back to a war zone, many of my ex-POW compatriots were eager to return to Java. They were the professional soldiers, planters, businessmen, postal clerks, teachers, and shopkeepers who wanted to see their homes and families. I feared going back there; it was the last thing I wanted. Holland was my home. Besides, I knew that my parents would soon be repatriated.

Although my days were full, I continued to be addicted to an hour's bedtime reading before going to sleep (this developed into a lifelong habit). I had stumbled upon the works of Multatuli, the nineteenth-century Dutch author who, in his day, had been at the center of a political storm. Multatuli was the pen name of the solidly Dutch Eduard Douwes Dekker, one of the first to draw attention to the inequities of the colonial system. In protest against the appalling conditions in which the Javanese lived, and their exploitation by the colonial masters, Dekker resigned his post in the civil service and returned to Holland to devote the rest of his life to writing and lecturing. I was fascinated by Multatuli's novel *Max Havelaar*, which I had bought at a bookstall near the newspaper and which came in a tattered eight-volume set. I wrote down on a piece of paper the words of "Saidah's Song," a poem in the book about a Javanese man contemplating the moment of his death. The first line at the start of each stanza went: "I don't know where I'll die . . ." I had no idea why I carried it around in my pocket, for I truly believed that I did not want to be reminded of Spring Camp.

Being obliged to print statements issued by the Dutch government about the situation in Indonesia on "my" front page, and meeting inexperienced Dutch officers and bureaucrats en route to (what they still considered to be) the Dutch East Indies, I was prompted to vent my own frustration on the people back home. I wrote a letter to the editor of the *Nieuwe Rotterdamsche Courant*, a leading newspaper in Holland, saying that it was my impression that the current authorities in Holland and their Indonesia-bound emissaries were wholly unequipped to cope with an entirely new set of conditions: large segments of the Indonesian population expressing their wish to throw off colonial rule and claiming their country's right to independence. To my surprise, the letter was quoted in a front-page editorial and sparked off a flood of angry letters asking what right a young whippersnapper like me had, sticking his nose into matters of state and undermining a righteous cause.

Regularly recurring bouts of malaria kept me out of the office for three to four days each month. My new friends, the Anglo-Hungarian physicians, prescribed various pills. Nothing worked. I was immune even to the newest antimalarial drugs. It was as if for each step forward, I took two backward. During the days that I ran a high temperature, sweat covered my face as if I was holding it under a showerhead. I was sternly told that the only way in which I could get rid of my feeling of illness and yellow-colored appearance was to return to Holland's temperate climate. I rejected the advice. I didn't care how I felt or looked. Life in Singapore was just too exciting.

In the fall of 1945 the Dutch liner *New Amsterdam*, en route to repatriating the first batch of Dutch civilians from Java, dropped anchor outside Singapore Harbor. Having received a message that my parents were aboard, I managed to talk my way onto a small boat (formerly a British customs vessel) that was taking a group of officials to the ship. Mother was overwhelmed with emotion when she saw me. She cried for most of the two hours I spent with her and Father on board the ship. Father remained composed but held my hand in both of his for a long time. I was taken aback by the way they looked: both now in their fifties, they acted old, far beyond their years. Mother's hair had turned completely white. They were as skinny and sickly as the survivors of the railroad. Father had not only lost a lot of weight; his eyes were watery and hollow. The three of us put up a brave front. Each said that we had come through well and that our imprisonment had not been that bad. I asked them if they knew any of the courageous Eurasian women who had been beheaded for trying to smuggle messages into the POW camps. I asked them if they had been beaten. But they did not want to talk about it. The only thing that Mother complained about was the lack of soap. (Later, when we were reunited in Holland, the subject never came up again. I must confess that I never pressed them very hard, for during their lifetime I was as reluctant to volunteer information as they were).

We just stared at each other, at a loss for words. But when I said to Father that my game of bridge had improved, he smiled for the first time. Mother wanted me to go back to Holland with them, right then and there. I promised that I would follow at the very earliest opportunity.

I seriously intended to keep my promise, but living the good life in Singapore, I kept procrastinating, even though the recurring attacks of malaria continued to sap my strength. Singapore had reassumed its multicolored, cosmopolitan hue; in addition to its native Chinese, there were thousands of Malays who had come down the causeway from Johore, along with thousands more Indian, British, and Australian troops, as well as the ex-POWs, still emaciated but now neatly uniformed. As I moved among different groups of friends, it became even harder to think of leaving. There was glamour in the journalists' world: most British, American, Australian, and French war correspondents stopped off at the *Straits Times* offices, and often I was invited to join them for a drink or a meal or a party.

On Friday nights I returned to Nussbaum, whose swelling congregation included newly arrived members of British and Dutch military personnel. My new Anglo-Hungarian doctor friends accompanied me to the services. The rest of the week, they and others in our building kept me up late, filling me in on what had been happening in the world at large during my three and a half years of isolation, when all information I received had been based as much on rumor as on the occasional clandestine summary of radio bulletins.

Some of my new British army friends had participated in the battles of North Africa and Italy; others had landed in Normandy shortly after D day; but most were fresh recruits on their first military mission outside their native country. The newcomers all took the position that a POW should be constantly on the lookout for an opportunity to escape. The veteran ex-prisoners and I listened warily when one of these greenhorns, a bright-eyed kid, only a few years younger in age but decades younger in experience than myself, argued passionately that it was better to die than to give up one's freedom. I kept quiet, remembering how idealistic I too had been at the outbreak of war in May 1940. My ordeal on the railroad had made me grow up. I now knew that wartime heroics were nothing but an abstract theory that had little to do with the physical and psychological realities I had been forced to face.

In Singapore I was no longer confronted with the seriously injured and the deadly sick ex-POWs. The one-armed, one-legged, scurvied, and otherwise maimed victims of Japanese mistreatment had been evacuated to their home countries as quickly as possible. What I did not realize was that some of the worst scars were mental, and therefore invisible. Two British medical studies published in 1990 reported that even after forty-five years, former prisoners had above-average levels of psychiatric illness and significantly higher rates of admission to hospitals. Thousands were suffering from psychological disorders from which they would never recover. A British magazine wrote that "it is widely felt that, even amongst the body of men who exhibit no clinical symptoms, their quality of life and indeed their longevity have been drastically reduced by their wartime experiences."

Many years later, shortly after the end of the Gulf War in 1990, I met one of these seriously traumatized ex-POWs at a business lunch in Holland. After exchanging pleasantries, we discovered that both of us had been in Changi. My neighbor suddenly brought his napkin to his eyes. "I often burst into tears," he said. "It happens at the drop of a hat; there's no way to stop it, and it usually occurs at an awkward moment." Recently, he said, he had been watching TV with his family when some footage came on of a handful of Iraqi soldiers captured by the Americans. It showed the Iraqis stretching out their arms toward the victorious American soldiers in a gesture of fear and despondency. "When I saw those Iraqis, I started to sob," my companion said, "much to my own embarrassment."

For a while I kept in touch with Willem, my old friend from camp. He had fallen in love with a Singapore woman whose husband had been killed in a Japanese massacre. He decided to take her and her child back to Java at the earliest opportunity. He wasn't too eager to go back to his old job as postal clerk in Bandung, however. "If matters settle down over there, I'll take my bride back to Java," he said. "But if Indonesia goes independent, I'll look you up in Holland."

My parents were back home, staying with a niece in Zandvoort, a resort town on the coast. The niece and her husband — Max and Lies Maarssen — had lost their parents and other relatives in the Holocaust. During the war, the young couple and their two children had gone into hiding. But now the whole family had picked up the pieces again. Father's letters spoke of happy gatherings. Cousin Dick, with whom I had begun my adventures, was also staying there, reunited with Ro, his mother. Dick had spent the war years as a Japanese prisoner of war on Sumatra; Ro had been in the same civilian camp as Mother. John, her husband, had died in the camp.

The news about the rest of Father's family was not good. Three aunts, sisters of Father's, their husbands, and all their children, with one lonely exception, had perished in the gas chambers. I realized that my grandparents had been lucky to have died a natural death before the war. Jaap, one of my companions in the plane-spotting days of May 1940, had also been killed. Many other friends also failed to return from the concentration camps. Among them was Jules van Hessen, who had sat next to me in school. Edith, his little sister (who was to become my wife) had survived by living under a false identity with a family of courageous anti-Nazis.

Father described Mother's birthday party, with the family all gathered around the piano. Max had a strong baritone and sang some of Father's favorite arias by Rossini and Verdi; Lies charmed her audience with French chansons. I pictured a refuge — warm and full of happy togetherness. Father's letters urged me to consider my various options for a field of study. He asked whether I was still interested in applying to Rotterdam's School of Economics. He enclosed a newspaper clipping about a new department at the University of Amsterdam offering a degree in the social and political sciences. It was to be called the Seventh Faculty. "This might be right up your alley," he wrote. He made it quite clear that he expected me to go to university. I was not so sure — I believed that the world was changing and that years of study might be a waste of time.

Meanwhile, the novelty of working at the newspaper had begun to wear off. My job had become routine, the parties were no longer as exciting, and I was still suffering from malaria. I looked like a yellow skeleton, unable to put on more weight no matter how hard I tried. And try I did — wolfing down three hearty meals each day, supplemented by food stall snacks of fried bananas or grilled chicken satay.

Finally I made my decision. I put in a request to be repatriated to Holland. On February 8, 1946, I boarded the *Alcantara*, a Dutch troop carrier that was transporting Dutch soldiers and civilians back to Holland.

When she sailed from Singapore Harbor, the *Alcantara* was on a northerly course, hugging the west coast of Malaysia. We proceeded in the same direction as the railroad tracks along which the Japanese had transported H-Force to Thailand. I looked back at the city where I had been a prisoner and at the coastline, my route to the Railway to Death. I felt a keen regret for the lost years of my life, but also a perverse pride — I had survived.

Every day at noon I would climb up to the bridge, from which I'd broadcast the day's news by bullhorn to the crowd below. As the ship's only journalist, I had been asked to translate the BBC bulletins into Dutch. The news was received in silence, but a loud cheer would go up when I announced the arrest of a Japanese indicted for war crimes.

On two postwar trips to Indonesia, I tried to find Willem, with little success. Willem had vanished, leaving no trace. The post office, his former employer, had no record of where he had gone. Then, in the early 1950s, a haunting thing happened. Edith and I were living in New York. During rush hour we were on a subway platform at one of Manhattan's busiest stops: the station at Forty-second Street and Times Square. The doors of the subway car opened, and a crowd of tourists and commuters surged toward us. Beyond them, inside the car we were trying to enter, I found myself looking directly at Willem, my mate, the one with whom I had made hundreds of rock-hauling trips up a hill by the river Kwai! I started to move toward him but was pushed back by a crush of people shoving their way out of the car. I shouted, "Willem!" His arm went straight up in a salute. The doors closed before my nose, and the train moved away. I never saw Willem again.

The sparse contacts I maintained with the few POWs I had found back after the war slowly evaporated. A few years ago I participated in a radio program of the Canadian Broadcasting Company in which tribute was paid to the courage of Chaim Nussbaum, who had emigrated to Toronto shortly after the war. I had seen him when he visited New York, a frail old man who bore only a slight resemblance to the young chaplain who had been such a charismatic preacher. In the mid-1980s, on a business visit to Canberra, Australia, I found an issue of *Habeemah* in that city's War Museum. A curator telephoned George Sprod, and two nights later, forty years after the end of the war, George and I met in the bar of my Sydney hotel. On my frequent visits to Amsterdam, I sometimes looked up Lex Noyon, now a retired professor of social science. I do not know what happened to Mose and whether he is still writing to Joshua.

In 1985, forty years after Japan's surrender, I finally found an opportunity to attend the annual reunion of the Dutch military survivors of the railroad. The reunion was held in a large hall in Utrecht, in the center of Holland. I was surrounded by tanned and wrinkled men in their sixties and seventies, many of whom wore regimental ties, tweeds, or dark blazers. After the formal part of the program — a number of boring and whining speeches — we were to gather in small groups to meet old friends. Veterans of various camps would meet under banners bearing the names of the camps along the railroad where we had lived and worked, and where many of our mates had died.

The man next to me explained that the number of
active members of the veterans' organization was dwindling rapidly.

I went over to the sign that read SPRING CAMP, clearly
painted in bold black letters. I waited for half an hour as
people collected under the other banners. No one else
showed up.

Epilogue

THE JAPANESE COMMANDING OFFICER of our captivity was convicted as a war criminal and put to death. Two Korean guards were also killed by a mob of angry Allied soldiers roaming the streets of Singapore in the aftermath of our liberation. Yet only a handful of Japanese military leaders and Japanese prison guards were arrested and indicted as war criminals. Less than fifty were convicted, and of those, few were sent to jail and even fewer executed. The officers and men of the Japanese army were quietly reabsorbed into the farms, factories, and offices of the home country. Japan showed neither defiance nor remorse. There was not the slightest concession of guilt. No one apologized, and few were held accountable. I convinced myself that the entire Japanese nation had overlooked, papered over, trivialized, or forgotten the atrocities committed in the name of its emperor. The country quietly embraced its returning soldiers as heroes; the Japanese nation felt victimized. The atomic attacks on Hiroshima and Nagasaki were the ultimate injustice. No Japanese seemed able to admit that an enemy might have suffered, too. No blame could be laid at their own door.

On the last day of my ocean voyage home, I gazed for the second time in five years at the cliffs of Dover, only now my ship was headed in the opposite direction, straight for the Dutch coast, from which I had fled in the *Zeemans Hoop* nearly six years earlier. A gray sky hung over the flat Dutch horizon; I could see the coastal towns strung along the North Sea shore, one of which was Scheveningen, the town where I had spent my youth. I was almost twenty-three now, but I felt like an old man. As the *Alcantara* entered the canal that connects the North Sea with the port of Amsterdam, every passenger was on deck. Wearing thin tropical clothes, the repatriates were chilled to the bone. I was shivering, not just with the cold but also with trepidation. We were grim and reflective. We were coming home to a country ravaged by war. I think every one of us dreaded the moment when the death of a loved one would be confirmed by a look in the eyes of relatives waiting for us onshore.

As I disembarked, I was conscious of being out of place. The air was not the air of the tropics. It wasn't the air of prewar Holland, either. The shabbiness of the people's clothes and the dilapidated buildings brought home how much had happened here while I was away. Nor was I the boy who had left six years ago. The taste of war still hung around me. It had permeated my mind; my skin color was yellow, and my breath smelled of the medicines that had so far failed to have any effect on my chronic malaria.

Father and Mother were waiting for me at the dock. Father's hand was raised in a frozen welcoming gesture. Mother clutched a handkerchief, tears in her eyes. They both were bundled up in warm coats. Before even kissing or hugging me, Mother immediately helped me into a heavy overcoat that enveloped me like a badly wrapped parcel. I must have looked even worse to them than I had during our brief reunion in the harbor of Singapore. I was a scrawny, yellow, sickly-looking youngster, only a shadow of my former self.

Life in postwar Holland, as I had already gathered from the radio and the newspaper clippings Father sent to me in Singapore, was depressing and gloomy. After the relative abundance of food in Singapore and the plentiful meals aboard ship, I was about to experience rationing: not only of food, but of clothing, shoes, and just about every other commodity. We had no home to return to. My parents and our other surviving relatives lived together in close quarters in the modest-sized house of my cousin Lies, her husband Max, and their two young children. The desperate housing shortage meant I was not going to get the privacy I so longed for after five years of prison and army life.

At six o'clock in the evening you would always find me near a radio for the BBC news. I was anxious to know when the war crimes trials would start, so that my captors might be brought to trial. The lack of progress in arresting or indicting my oppressors was frustrating. I didn't want to listen to the endless arguments about how best to bring war criminals to justice, and about which ones should be prosecuted and which ones allowed to go free. I felt the seething rage that had taken hold of me on the night march out of Bangpong, when our Japanese guards committed the gross injustice of shortening our rest period. This time there was nothing to stop me from venting my anger; I could kick and punch the walls and curse to my heart's content. Not that it made any difference.

I began a new life. At the University of Amsterdam I met Edith van Hessen, the younger sister of my old schoolmate Jules, one of my many prewar friends who had not survived. Jules had gone underground in 1942 to flee the Nazis. He found work as a farmhand, moving from one farm to the next, and was preparing to escape to England by boat when he was arrested and sent to a concentration camp. When I bumped into Edith at the university (we were both taking the same oversubscribed course, given by a popular philosopher, Professor Henk Pos), I asked her what had happened to Jules. She told me that he had died in Auschwitz-Birkenau after two botched escape attempts.

I met her again at the wedding of a mutual friend in Rotterdam. We danced and fell in love. A year later, Edith left for the United States to do graduate work in psychology at Columbia University. I was impatient, and cajoled and begged her to return to Holland so that we might get married. When she finally relented and returned to Amsterdam (after what seemed an interminable absence but had actually been only nine months!), I promised to take her back to America at the earliest opportunity.

Life in the Netherlands in the late 1940s was difficult both physically and psychologically. Almost the entire population carried the burden of the war's memory, collectively and individually. Apart from the mental wounds that had not yet healed, our standard of living bore no resemblance to what we had been used to in our comfortable bourgeois prewar existence. So the idea of emigrating to the United States held considerable appeal. It took several months before we obtained our visas, settled our Dutch taxes, and finished saying our long good-byes to my parents and our friends. But finally, fifteen months after our wedding, the proud parents of twin girls, we disembarked in Hoboken to start a new life. We were determined to leave the past behind on the other side of the Atlantic.

Waiting at the dock to welcome us to New York was Guus, Edith's elder brother. He had been sent to the United States shortly before the German invasion to learn the lumber trade. He had enlisted in the U.S. Army and had been one of the first soldiers to liberate Maastricht, Holland's southernmost city. After the war he had returned to the United States, where he bought a lumber mill in Maryland.

It was a hot and humid day. The oppressive heat, so

different from the moderate climate of Holland, brought back memories of my sweaty years in Southeast Asia. Hundreds of people were milling around in the moist, tearful, and emotionally charged atmosphere. We called out our final good-byes to our shipboard friends and fellow immigrants, at the same time trying to hug Guus and his wife while struggling with two restless and unhappy babies. In the confusion, as I put my jacket back on while balancing one of the twins on my hip, I suddenly noticed that my wallet with our passports and travelers checks was missing. After a panicky half hour, an employee of the Holland America Line brought our lost documents back. It was not a very auspicious beginning to our new life in America.

On our way to Baltimore, where my in-laws lived, we stopped off at a Howard Johnson's, the first child-friendly restaurant we had ever encountered. I was dazzled by the menu, but Edith claimed to be disappointed: the number of ice cream flavors on offer had been reduced by half since her last visit in 1948. After a few months in Baltimore to get acclimatized, we moved to an apartment in Queens because I had decided that New York was the place to be. It took me at least half a year to get accustomed to the sounds, smells, and sights of the city. I was overwhelmed by the contrasts — the bustling metropolis compared to which Amsterdam now seemed to me downright provincial; the tall, gleaming buildings contrasted to the medieval canal houses; the prosperity of the New World, so different from the postwar shabbiness of the Old World;

the heartiness and openness of the people compared with the cowed, dour mood of the war-scarred Dutch. We had been liberated; but this was truly the land of the free.

In Amsterdam I had been working as senior editor and supervisor of the art department for a publishing company that specialized in industrial house organs. In that capacity, I worked closely with some of Holland's largest printers, who, when it became known that I was emigrating to the United States, offered to appoint me as their American sales representative. In making the rounds of New York publishers, I learned to my chagrin that no one in the publishing world seemed to be aware of the Dutch claim that a certain Laurens Janszoon Koster had invented the printing press in the fifteenth century! New Yorkers, it seemed, only recognized Johannes Gutenberg, on whom the Germans had bestowed the title of inventor and founder of the printing industry. They had never even heard of Koster!

It occurred to me that to improve the Dutch printing industry's chances in the States, it would be useful to publicize its historical origins. I went in search of a venue like the Library of Congress, to mount an exhibition vaunting the Dutch presses' long and illustrious history. While in this pursuit, I stumbled upon the American concept of "public relations," a term unknown not only in Holland but in the rest of Europe as well. When John Hill, the founder of the PR firm Hill and Knowlton and my future boss, visited Paris in 1952 on behalf of a U.S. client and went looking for a local office to work with, he was amazed to find out that PR consultancies did not exist in France.

My entry to Hill and Knowlton was as much of a fluke as many other events in my life. Over supper one night in New York, I had a discussion with Leon Lipson, a young lawyer and one of my closest friends, about the dispute between the Netherlands and Indonesia over the status of Irian Jaya, the western half of New Guinea, which the Indonesians claimed as an integral part of their archipelago and the Dutch proposed as an independent state (more or less under Holland's tutelage). The following day Leon introduced me to George Ball, a senior partner in his law firm (Ball later joined the government and ended his career as secretary of state in the Johnson administration).

"Leon tells me that you think you know why the Dutch lost their case on Irian before the Security Council," Mr. Ball said. "Tell me about it." I suggested that if the Dutch had done a better PR job, it might have helped their case. "The Dutch government did not understand much about American public opinion," I said, as if I had great insight into such matters. Ball encouraged me to continue. "Americans favor the underdog," I further pontificated. "They have a great deal of sympathy for the Indonesians who want their country's independence, whereas they hold no great affection for those old colonial Dutch who want to lord it over the poor and oppressed." I ended by saying, "The Dutch should have tried to gain the American public's understanding and sympathy in a major public relations campaign. They were wrong in thinking that by merely having their ambassador put forward some legal and historic arguments before the United Nations Security Council, they would win their case."

The next major debate at the United Nations happened to be on Morocco (a jewel in France's colonial crown). Ball's firm represented the French government in its efforts to scuttle that country's attempt to gain independence from France. "Write up what you just told me," Ball said. "We'll pay you two hundred dollars." And so I had my first paying PR assignment. As it turned out, my analysis was sent on to the French Ministry of Foreign Affairs but was never acted upon — a fate only too common in the consulting business! (For the record, France, like the Netherlands, lost its case before the UN.)

While in Paris, looking for a European PR counsel, Hill happened to meet the resident partner of Ball's firm. "There's a young Dutchman living in New York who is doing some kind of PR work for our firm," he informed Hill. Several months later Hill called and invited me to see him. "What do you know about PR?" he asked me. "Nothing," I said. "Good," said Hill. "You're hired."

I was excited to join Hill and Knowlton, at that time (and for years to come) the largest and most influential PR firm in America. I liked living in America; I was embarking on a new career, I had regained my strength and no longer suffered from the sweats brought on by malaria. Life was good. I tried not to give the war years another thought.

That was easier said than done, however. Sometimes I would wake up in the middle of the night in a cold sweat, visualizing the graveyard of Spring Camp and vividly remembering the corpse that I had dropped because it had been too heavy to carry. Then I would walk over to the cots of my two children, watch them breathe and smack their lips in their sleep, and feel restored. But the full force of my past came back to haunt me sooner than I expected.

A few months after joining the firm, I was thrown into the deep end when I was told I was being sent on the firm's first overseas assignment. I was to be part of a two-man team sent to the Middle and Far East to conduct a three-month survey of the public relations needs of Caltex, the international oil company, in Bahrain, India, the Philippines, Indonesia, and . . . Japan.

When I learned that the Caltex assignment would include Tokyo, I asked to speak to Hill. "I don't think I can take this one on; sorry. I'm an ex-POW," I reminded him.

Hill was blunt. "This is your big chance," he said. "And I think you're a bigger man than you think. You have twenty-four hours to think it over." I took the job.

The Tokyo of 1953, one year after the American occupation had ended, was home to few Americans or Europeans. In the rush hour, its streets became a human stampede. I felt lost and isolated, the only non-Japanese face in the crowd. The city was gray, in contrast to New York or London or Amsterdam, its people one dark-hued homogeneous mass that went rapidly but quietly about its business. It was eight years after the end of the war, but fire-ravaged areas and half-destroyed, burned-out buildings were still in evidence. A massive rebuilding was under way. Towering cranes were visible everywhere. Here and there sat a white-clad war veteran with a begging bowl in front of him. There was no laughter.

In the meetings that had been set up for me, I could not help wondering if my Japanese interlocutors were the brothers or comrades-in-arms of my former tormentors. Caltex was in partnership with a local oil company, whose Japanese executives showed little or no interest in being interviewed. Most of the information we were after could only be gleaned from the handful of Americans who had been put on our prearranged schedule. None of the Western expatriates seemed comfortable in their new environment. To me the whole atmosphere was cold and distant, quite a contrast to the much more hospitable and cooperative attitudes of the Indians, Indonesians, and Filipinos we had encountered on the preceding legs of our trip. One incident stuck in my mind. Passing an office, I heard a loud, barking voice. From the corner of my eye, in a fleeting moment, I glimpsed a sharply dressed senior Japanese official, to whom I had been introduced earlier, chew out a rather shabbily outfitted underling. Inevitably I speculated that the senior man was an ex-officer snapping an order to his corporal, who in turn would remove a hammer from his belt and plant it in the small of my back. I began to realize how deep the Japanese experience was buried beneath my skin.

In 1954 Hill called me into his office again. "I think the time has come to open an office in Europe. And I think you're the man to do it."

"But we haven't got a single client over there!" I protested.

"That'll be your job, young man," he drawled.

And so we found ourselves crossing the Atlantic again, on the *Queen Elizabeth I*, but with one big difference: this time, we were traveling first class, not steerage. After trying out Paris and The Hague, I eventually settled on Geneva as the most favorable location for an international headquarters.

Two decades later, at a time when Japan had emerged as an industrial powerhouse, I attended one of the first meetings that brought business executives from all the Pacific Basin nations together. At dinner in Kyoto, we were a mixed group: six men, one each from Australia, Canada, Mexico, Peru, Japan, and the United States. It was a pleasant social occasion: we went around the table telling one another about our backgrounds. Yet, hard as we tried to include him, our Japanese host, who spoke fluent English, would only respond with a sweet smile.

The following afternoon, during a long break, some of my colleagues and I went for a stroll in a nearby temple garden. We encountered a group of young girls in school uniform. In broken English their teacher told us that they were from a small town in the north and that her twelve-year-old pupils had never seen a Caucasian in the flesh. It explained the girls' giggles and snickers. One of our group invited the youngsters to pose for a group picture. They happily consented. The experience was a refreshing break from our tense discussions on the often otherwise dull subjects of import quotas and government subsidies. It was now 1974. Encountering another face of Japan made me realize that to encompass all Japanese in my visceral reaction was neither fair nor helpful. From that day on I began to draw a distinction between the prewar generation of Japanese — those of my own age — and the contemporaries of my children, born after the war.

Also in the mid-1970s, in Tokyo, three *salrymen* (business executives) introduced me to the rites of the geisha house. It was an elegant occasion, where an ornately made-up and elaborately costumed young woman fed me delicate morsels of food and an infinite number of cups of sake. My Japanese hosts laughed and flirted; one of the women played the lute, another sang with a birdlike voice. After dinner, my friends took me to a bar on the Ginza, Tokyo's entertainment district. Inside, an all-male, middle-age crowd was belting out songs, fully lubricated with sake, whiskey, and brandy. After a while it struck me that they seemed to be singing the same melody over and over. They would end the song with a thunderous cheer, and then launch into the same refrain all over again, with the volume turned up another notch. It sounded very jovial. I kept tipsily asking for a translation. I assumed that when these buttoned-down, white-shirted, and up-tight technocrats finally let down their hair, there was bound to be some good off-color stuff. My Japanese chaperons giggled, but ignored my request. I persisted. Finally I got my answer. The man who gave it had his mouth set in a frozen grin. The song was quite proper, he said, and not at all what I thought. It was a highly patriotic song, a military march, written to keep up morale and sung on memorable occasions — as when the Japanese fleet was steaming toward Pearl Harbor. I bowed, and thanked him for the information. Suddenly, I was stone-cold sober.

Eventually I was invited to a private home. It was the first time this had happened in my twenty-five years of visiting Japan. My host, the chairman of a powerful advertising agency, was a colorful character who exploded the myth of all Japanese businessmen being one gray, indistinguishable mass. He cherished two passionate hobbies: motorcycles and cookery. My wife and I were shown into the elegant living space of a roomy home furnished with highly polished, sawed-down Louis XV furniture. At the far end of the room was a counter at which we were seated to observe our host display his culinary skills. Our host prepared each dish very carefully. He worked alone, his wife assisting only in serving us a succession of tempura courses. Neither of them sat down to eat with us. We were offered a never-ending array of exotic and exquisite deep-fried, bite-sized morsels of tuna, prawn, oyster, meats, vegetables, and flowers. Towards the end of the meal I felt emboldened to ask how the chairman had fared during the war.

"Please have another chrysanthemum," he said cryptically.

Over the course of time I got a little more used to the Japanese. Our company had bought a small Japanese consulting firm in Tokyo, and I visited Japan at least one a year. I had learned to appreciate my Japanese business contacts as extremely smart and polite people. In negotiations they proved to be tough and often stubborn, but in the after-office hours they were a civilized lot, always correct with an occasional flash of kindness. I was invited to classical concerts and the Kabuki theater, with its graphic depiction of conflict between the noble and humane against power-hungry evil. There was no longer any reason to think of the Japanese as the bad guys. Yet I never lost my compulsion to keep a wary eye on them.

In 1974, having been instrumental in setting up Hill and Knowlton's international network, I returned to New York, where I eventually assumed the position of chairman and chief executive officer of the U.S. and worldwide operations. I had served nineteen years in Europe and had also been responsible for supervising the Tokyo office. But my dealings with the Japanese did not end there. When talk of a U.S.-Japan "trade war" created an urgent need throughout the business community for public relations advice on dealing with Japan, I became focused on the country once again.

Some forty years after the end of the war, I was seated in a comfortable armchair on a high floor of a modern Tokyo office building. Facing me was the president of Mitsui, one of Japan's most powerful conglomerates: a pleasant, round-faced, and soft-spoken man. We were cochairing a task force of Japanese and American businessmen that was to look into ways of improving communications between our two countries. It all seemed so simple: devise effective communication, and better understanding would follow. I looked cautiously at my host. He sent me a faint smile. What were his thoughts about the West, and about Japan's defeat in the war?

An aide walked in, bowed deeply in my direction, and handed his boss a note. The chairman excused himself for the interruption and left the room. Returning after about ten minutes, he said, "We have a crisis in Madagascar. No matter, we will have it all under control very soon." He added: "We have excellent intelligence all over the world." Inevitably, my thoughts strayed to the quality of Japanese intelligence prior to World War II, when Japanese residents of Southeast Asia (in contrast to the unfairly interned Japanese Americans) had turned out to be effective spies for the Japanese invaders.

I had finally learned, to my great frustration, that World War II was a topic not to be discussed with foreigners. For the Japanese, the war was treated as an intimate family album: its pictures were to be shown only to family members, and as presented in the bland history books used in Japanese schools. When it came to wartime behavior, the Japanese appeared to be suffering from a case of collective amnesia. Under no circumstance was blame to be ascribed to any Japanese, dead or alive.

As a speaker at a meeting on trade held in Hakone, an elegant lakeside resort within easy driving distance of Tokyo, my presentation dealt with the American public's attitudes toward economically successful Japan, which had conquered the U.S. automobile, TV, and electronic markets while protecting its own turf from foreign imports. Looking out at the large audience in a sumptuous brightly lighted hall, I noticed that the Japanese delegation formed a solid, stone-faced mass. I needed a moment to collect myself — I suddenly saw the faces of my prison guards before me. Then I shook myself and regained my self-confidence. I became overconfident and began to take satisfaction in haranguing them on their failures. I doubted that I was getting through, but I did not care. In the discussion afterward each side remained convinced of the righteousness of its own position. The two points of view were diametrically opposed. The culture gap remained wide and deep.

Gradually I learned to feel more comfortable, especially in one-on-one encounters. But it had taken me more than thirty-five years to reach this point. Now and then, I must confess, I did enjoy a little schadenfreude, especially when the Chinese, Koreans, Filipinos, and other Southeast Asians made it clear, time and again, that they had neither forgiven nor forgotten the behavior of the Japanese during the war.

Several years ago Edith and I rode a tourist bus through central Java. Our fellow visitors were all Americans. None of them had even the remotest personal tie to Indonesia. By contrast, we, as native-born Dutch, felt great sentimental affinity toward the Indonesians. We therefore squirmed in our seats when, in answer to a question about Indonesia's history, our English-speaking guide condemned his country's long Dutch colonial era as an unforgettable period of deprivation and humiliation. At a rest stop we confessed to our guide that we were Dutch natives. We then asked whether his village had suffered from Dutch domination and oppression. He smiled broadly and said in fluent Dutch: "I am so happy to speak your language again, *meneer, mevrouw*. Let me tell you. Three and a half years of Japanese occupation were far worse than three hundred years of Dutch colonial rule."

EPILOGUE

In the 1990s the Japanese economy passed into a long period of serious decline. Japan's economic crisis left the world flummoxed once again: How could this have happened? How could the Japanese have fooled us all along about their economic strength? Why weren't we smart enough to foresee the collapse?

Of course, very few thinkers and analysts ever get it right. No one predicted the rise and fall of Hitler's Germany either. We in the West have been consistently wrong, always shortsighted in our judgment of political and economic trends. No one foresaw the rapid collapse of the Soviet Union, nor that the dot-com boom would end up being a bust. Western businessmen had for a long time been dazzled by the success of Japanese industry. We had even tried to copy some Japanese business methods: quality-control circles and on-time delivery systems became accepted practices and entered the business lexicon. Most of us did not pay much attention to the intrinsic weaknesses of the Japanese system. The intertwined, incestuous relationship between business and government had been largely responsible for Japan's economic victories. We knew all about that. But we knew little, and understood less, of one of its main downsides: the banking system's habit of extending, with the government's blessing, huge amounts of credit to a large number of enterprises that were neither destined to grow nor, at a later time, able to cope with a slowdown in demand. This tight collusion between government, industry, and bankers created what came to be known as Japan, Inc. The government also kept up an illusion of economic and financial solidity by subsidizing Japan's small and backward but politically powerful rice growers, and by spending great amounts of money on roads that led nowhere, as well as on all sorts of other superfluous public construction projects. At the same time, Japan, Inc. shut all foreign competitors out of its domestic market by erecting high tariff walls, while the Japanese equivalent of our Federal Reserve was skillfully manipulating the yen-dollar exchange rate to assist Japanese exports. In the end, of course, the whole house of cards came crashing down.

With the emergence of China as a major player on the world stage, Western voices have begun expressing the hope that Japan will reconsider its assumption that it is the most powerful and only real pace-setting nation on the Asian continent. It is encouraging to note that many in Japan's postwar generation are open to that view. But I feel we must always remember that we have been here before. All too frequently, the West has thought that Japan was becoming less isolated from the rest of the world. (All too often, it seems to me, our eagerness to see change has colored our judgment and made us overly optimistic.) I am also reminded that at a time of great human misery, resulting in large migratory waves, Japan remains the only prosperous industrialized country nearly hermetically closed to refugees and allows only a handful of foreign residents each year to acquire Japanese citizenship. Other countries worry about being able to handle the successful integration of large-scale immigration; only Japan seems more motivated by a desire to preserve its individuality and self-imposed insularity. And despite protests from the Asian nations that suffered under the Japanese occupation, leading Japanese politicians, including the current and last prime ministers, insist on making the annual pilgrimage to a shrine that honors Japan's wartime leaders.

Most of the POWs, my Japanese guards, and my older Japanese business contacts are now dead. The *Zeemans Hoop* has long since been turned into scrap metal. Spring Camp has become jungle once more, although Changi Gaol still stands (it is now Singapore's high-security prison). Soon there will be no one left to remember, no one left to apologize to. The current generation of young Japanese (grandchildren of my contemporaries) is more open and communicative than their parents' and grandparents' generation. My friend Lex, with whom I shared a cell in Changi, was comforted by a conversation he had with Japanese students near the bank of the river Kwai. They were curious to know what had happened during the war and seemed skeptical of their elders' version, which claimed that the railway had had the noble purpose of making a significant and lasting contribution to the Thai economy!

Perhaps one day these younger Japanese will take a cue from the heirs to Germany's Nazi regime, who have demonstrated that frankness and repentance will go a long way toward diminishing mutual prejudices and helping to restore faith and trust among peoples. Whether America erred or was justified in using the atomic bomb, it has certainly gone out of its way to express regret and remorse for the horror it unleashed on two Japanese cities and the Japanese nation as a whole. So far, the Japanese have failed to reciprocate.

Some years ago, I participated in a role-playing exercise in which a small group of Americans was assigned to act like Japanese, and the Japanese like Americans. It came as no great surprise to me that neither side was able to successfully impersonate the other: the Americans were too boisterous to find the right tone; the Japanese squirmed at playing tough. We laughed a lot, but I realized that it would take a long time before Westerners and Japanese would be cured of their incompatibility.

I have often wondered what strange twist of fate led me to become a participant in the messy late-twentieth-century U.S.-Japanese trade controversy (as a consultant and a member of a bilateral U.S.-Japan organization). It may be that, as a former POW, I felt I possessed some insight my amiable, generous, and often less experienced American colleagues lacked. It might also have helped that for more than thirty years I had constantly shifted gears from one culture to the next; often speaking in and listening to three or four different languages several times in the course of a single day. I had become an itinerant outsider. All that might have contributed to my coming to terms with my more unpleasant memories. It also forced me to shake hands with my former oppressors and made it necessary for me to try to understand their position.

I offer my story, therefore, not as a cautionary tale, but as the observations and reminiscences of a single witness to a chapter of World War II that has been all but forgotten. I hope that when my grandchildren, and perhaps their children's children, read it, the lack of understanding between our cultures will have become a thing of the past.

I believe that one day this may really happen — but only after each side proves itself willing to acknowledge its own shortcomings. Then both sides must also be prepared to abolish the prejudices that still linger. As for my own generation, we Westerners share with our former Japanese enemies and adversaries the commonality of death, which will extinguish all manifestations of national pride and racial distinction.

Acknowledgments

WHEN I BECAME A PRISONER I got into the habit of taking notes. I scribbled these down on pads and sheets of colored paper. Later, when times turned tough, I used any scrap I could lay hands on. Later still, when I had shrunk into a walking skeleton clinging on to the barest of possessions, I lost the lot. I had neither the courage nor the stamina to resume taking notes. I no longer wished to record the atrocities happening around me.

What I have now written is largely based on memory. I started the process when I retired. Many memories had stayed with me; they were like implants in my brain. Others I found near the surface, often lurking just below a façade of cheerful optimism. I could recall them at the drop of a hat. Yet others would reappear as I emerged from a deep night's sleep or an afternoon's slumber on my favorite sofa. And then there were those that lay buried deep down inside me. These were harder to recover: images, sounds, and smells, even tastes, all eclipsed for decades.

As my main editor, my daughter Hester encouraged me to abandon a life-long practice of writing dry and often dull business memos and reports for a more writerly style. One important suggestion she made was difficult to follow. "Let your guard down," she said. "Show your emotions." Marianne, her twin sister and a publisher said: "Peel off the layers." Both admonishments were respectfully accepted. Still, baring my emotions was easier said than done.

So I wrote and with Hester's help re-wrote several drafts, determined to leave for my children and grandchildren a record of what happened to me in World War II. In doing so, I followed in the footsteps of Edith, who wrote a book about "her" World War that was published some years ago. She was the one who insisted that I should not abandon the project, especially during the dark days when I had had enough of delving into the painful past. This book would not have been written without the encouragement of Edith and Hester.

I am grateful to Ronald Searle for granting me permission to use some of his wartime drawings.

I also want to thank two friends: Jon Swan who read, gave his comments and edited an early version, as well as Leo Goldberger, my walking partner. Leon referred my manuscript to Richard Seaver, president and editor in chief of Arcade, who has given me important editorial advice.